Abingdon's

BibleZONE®

Where the Bible Comes to Life

Preschool   10

Jesus Christ:
What a Story!

Also available from
— Abingdon Press: —

Abingdon's BibleZone®
Preschool 10
FUNspirational® Kit

Abingdon's BibleZone®
Younger Elementary 10
Teacher's Guide
Abingdon's BibleZone®
Younger Elementary 10
FUNspirational® Kit

Abingdon's BibleZone®
Older Elementary 10
Teacher's Guide
Abingdon's BibleZone®
Older Elementary 10
FUNspirational® Kit

Writer/Editor: Daphna Flegal
Production Editors: Betsi Hoey Smith
and Leslie Johnson
Production and Design Manager:
R. E. Osborne
Designer: Paige Easter
Cover Photo: Sid Dorris
Illustrator: Robert S. Jones

Abingdon's

Bible ZONE

Preschool
10

Where the Bible Comes to Life

JESUS CHRIST: WHAT A STORY!

Abingdon Press
Nashville

Abingdon's
BibleZone®
Where the Bible Comes to Life
Preschool 10

99 00 01 02 03 04 05 06 07 08–10 9 8 7 6 5 4 3 2 1

MANUFACTURED IN THE UNITED STATES OF AMERICA

▼able of Contents

Jesus Christ: What a Story!

Bible Units in the ZONE

Use these suggestions if you choose to organize the lessons in short-term units.

1

Jesus—Nativity and Childhood

Bible Story	Bible Verse
In the Stable	A child is born to us! Isaiah 9:6, *Good News Bible*
By the Star's Light	A child is born to us! Isaiah 9:6, *Good News Bible*
With the Elders	Jesus grew both in body and in wisdom. Luke 2:52, *Good News Bible*

2

Jesus—His Ministry

Bible Story	Bible Verse
At the River	Jesus grew both in body and in wisdom. Luke 2:52, *Good News Bible*
In the Desert	Jesus grew both in body and in wisdom. Luke 2:52, *Good News Bible*
At the Synagogue	Jesus grew both in body and in wisdom. Luke 2:52, *Good News Bible*
By the Sea	And Jesus said to them, "Follow me." Mark 1:17

3

Jesus—Teachings

Bible Story	Bible Verse
On the Hillside	And Jesus said to them, "Follow me." Mark 1:17
Through the Roof	And Jesus said to them, "Follow me." Mark 1:17
With His Friends	And Jesus said to them, "Follow me." Mark 1:17

4

Jesus—Death and Resurrection

Bible Story	Bible Verse
Out of the Tomb	Sing for joy to the LORD. Psalm 98:4, *Good News Bible*
On the Road	Sing for joy to the LORD. Psalm 98:4, *Good News Bible*
With Us Always	And remember, I am with you always. Matthew 28:20.

About BibleZone

ZoneZillies:

ZoneZillies® are game and storytelling props found in the BibleZone® FUNspirational® Kit. Some ZoneZillies® are consumable and will need to be replaced. These are added for the teacher's convenience.

- smile face beanbag key chains
- smile face finger puppets
- inflatable feather pillow
- camel beanbag
- celestial ball
- prism star stickers
- star glitter wand (requires two AA batteries, not included)
- turkey basters
- sandpaper sheets
- ribbon
- Cassette with music by Brentwood Kids Music

Not recommended for children under 3.

Supplies:

- Bible
- cassette player
- two AA batteries
- construction paper
- glue
- safety scissors
- clear plastic tape
- masking tape
- stapler, staples
- crayons or markers
- chalk
- water
- paint drop cloth, old shower curtains, or large towels
- newspapers
- paper plates
- small and large paper bags
- paper towels
- tempera paint, paintbrushes
- shallow trays or box lids
- crayons with papers removed
- paint smocks
- drinking straws
- paper punch
- fabric, ribbon, or lace scraps
- glitter crayons or scented crayons
- Epsom salts
- shallow containers
- cotton balls, cotton swabs
- yarn or string
- basket or box
- dishpan
- hand-washing supplies
- small table or large box
- pillows, carpet samples, benches, or chairs
- rolled paper
- netting
- vegetable or fruit mesh bags
- spoons
- colored tissue paper
- mural paper
- sand
- sheet or towel

7

Where the Bible Comes to Life

Have fun learning about the life of Jesus. Each lesson in this teacher guide is filled with games and activities that will make learning FUNspirational® for you and your children. With just a few added supplies, everything you need to teach is included in Abingdon's BibleZone® FUNspirational® Kit. You may want to add BZ Bee, a colorful and plush hand puppet that the children will love (see page 174). BZ Bee helps teach the Bible verse each week in the *ZoneIn® with BZ Bee* section.

Each lesson has a ZoneIn® box:

> **ZONE IN**
> We celebrate with joy because we know Jesus is alive!

that is repeated over and over again throughout the lesson. The ZoneIn® states the Bible message in words your children will understand.

Use the following tips to help make your trip into the BibleZone® a FUNspirational® success!

- Read through each lesson. Read the Bible passages.
- Memorize the Bible verse and the ZoneIn® statement.
- Choose activities that fit your unique group of children and your time limitations.
- Practice telling the BibleZone® story.
- Gather the ZoneZillies® you will use for the lesson.
- Gather supplies you will use for the lesson.
- Learn the music for the lesson from the BibleZone® FUNspirational® Cassette.
- Arrange your room space to fit the lesson. Move tables and chairs so there is plenty of room for the children to move and to sit on the floor.
- Copy the Reproducible pages for the lesson.
- Copy the HomeZone® page for Parents.
- Copy the nametags (page 172), All About You page (page 173), and birthday banner (page 167) to use as needed with your class.

Preschoolers

Each child in your class is a one-of-a-kind child of God. Each child has his or her own name, background, family situation, and set of experiences. It is important to remember and celebrate the uniqueness of each child. Yet all of these one-of-a-kind children of God have some common needs.

- All children need love.
- All children need a sense of self-worth.
- All children need to feel a sense of accomplishment.
- All children need to have a safe place to be and to express their feelings.
- All children need to be surrounded by adults who love them.
- All children need to experience the love of God.

Preschoolers (children ages 3-5 years old) also have some common characteristics.

Their Bodies
- They do not sit still for very long.
- They have lots of energy.
- They enjoy moving (running, galloping, dancing, jumping, hopping).
- They are developing fine motor skills (learning to cut with scissors, learning to handle a ball, learning to tie their shoes).
- They enjoy using their senses (taste, touch, smell, hearing, seeing).

Their Minds
- They are learning more and more words.
- They enjoy music.
- They are learning to express their feelings.
- They like to laugh and be silly.
- They enjoy nonsense words.
- They are learning to identify colors, sizes, and shapes.
- They have an unclear understanding of time.
- They have a wonderful imagination.

Their Relationships
- They are beginning to interact with others as they play together.
- They are beginning to understand that other people have feelings.
- They are learning to wait for their turn.
- They can have a hard time leaving parents, especially mother.
- They want to help.
- They love to feel important.

Their Hearts
- They need to handle the Bible and see others handle it.
- They need caring adults who model Christian attitudes and behaviors.
- They need to sing, move to, and say Bible verses.
- They need to hear clear, simple stories from the Bible.
- They can express simple prayers.
- They can experience wonder and awe at God's world.
- They can share food and money and make things for others.
- They can experience belonging at church.

In the Stable

Enter the Zone

Bible Verse
A child is born to us!
Isaiah 9:6, *Good News Bible*

Bible Story
Luke 2:1–7

According to the Book of Luke, Mary and Joseph had to travel to Bethlehem to be counted for a census. Because Joseph was a descendent of David, and David's hometown was Bethlehem, Joseph and Mary traveled to Bethlehem.

Bethlehem was approximately ninety miles south of Nazareth, the home of Joseph and Mary. They probably made the journey on foot. It is possible that Mary did ride a donkey at least part of the way.

After a long, dusty journey they arrived in Bethlehem. The town was probably very crowded because of the census. So instead of being able to get a room in the inn, Joseph and Mary ended up staying in a stable with animals. It was here that Jesus was born.

The stable may have been part of the inn's courtyard, or it could have been inside a cave. There are many caves around Bethlehem that were used as stables in Biblical times. The animals were fed from a trough or manger. Mary laid baby Jesus in the feeding trough.

After Jesus was born, Mary would have washed him and rubbed his body with salt. Then she would have wrapped him in bands of soft cloth. These bands of cloth would completely encircle the baby's body. The purpose of the bands was to keep him warm and to help his body grow straight and strong. The bands would have been loosened several times a day, and the skin rubbed with olive oil and dusted with powdered myrtle leaves.

When God decided to send Jesus into the world, Jesus came as an ordinary person. He lived an ordinary life with ordinary parents. Jesus could therefore identify with the poor people of his day and with their struggles. How appropriate that Jesus' life story should begin in the humblest fashion—in an animal shelter.

We praise and thank God for Jesus.

Scope the ZONE

ZONE	TIME	SUPPLIES	⊙ ZILLIES®
Zoom Into the Zone			
Tambourine Tap	15 minutes	Reproducible 1A, safety scissors, crayons or markers, paper plates, glue, paper punch, tape	ribbon
Manger Millinery	10 minutes	Reproducible 1B, scissors, construction paper, crayons or markers, glue, tape or stapler and staples	none
BibleZone®			
Animal Antics	5 minutes	headbands (Reproducible 1B)	none
Sign 'n Say	5 minutes	none	none
In the Stable	10 minutes	headbands (Reproducible 1B)	none
Bible Verse Buzz	5 minutes	Bible, BZ Bee	none
Sing!	5 minutes	tambourines (Reproducible 1A), cassette player	Cassette
LifeZone			
Star Freeze	5 minutes	headbands (Reproducible 1B)	celestial ball
Star Games	10 minutes	none	celestial ball
Stable Song	5 minutes	none	none
Caravan Prayers	5 minutes	none	camel beanbag

⊙ Zillies® are found in the **BibleZone® FUNspirational® Kit.**

Zoom Into the Zone®

Choose one or more activities to catch your children's interest.

Supplies:
Reproducible 1A, safety scissors, crayons or markers, paper plates, glue, paper punch, tape

Zillies®:
ribbon

Tambourine Tap

Ⓟ hotocopy the Nativity circle **(Reproducible 1A)** for each child. Cut out the circles for younger children. Let older children cut out the circles themselves using safety scissors. Let the children decorate the pictures with crayons or markers.

Give each child a paper plate. Show the children how to glue the Nativity circles into the center of the plates. Let the children use a paper punch to punch holes around the edges of the plates.

Cut **ribbon** into two 18- to 24-inch lengths for each child. Wrap one end of each length with tape. Show the children how to weave the ribbon through the holes. Help each child tie off the ends of the ribbon. Leave any extra ribbon to make streamers hanging off the plates. Show the children how to tap the plates like you would tambourines.

Say: Today our Bible story is about when baby Jesus was born. Jesus was born to show God's love.

> **We praise and thank God for Jesus.**

Supplies:
Reproducible 1B, scissors, construction paper, crayons or markers, glue, tape or stapler and staples

Zillies®:
none

Manger Millinery

Ⓟ hotocopy the animal faces **(Reproducible 1B)** and cut out the ovals. You will need one animal for each child. Cut construction paper into halves lengthwise to make strips.

Let each child pick an animal face from the ovals. Encourage the children to decorate the animal faces with crayons or markers.

Give each child two strips of construction paper. Have the children glue or tape the ends of the strips together to make one long strip. Show each child how to glue the animal face oval onto the strip. Measure the strip around each child's head so that the animal face is in the front. Tape or staple the strip to make a headband. If you use staples, make sure the prongs are facing away from the children's heads.

Say: Jesus was born in a stable, a place for animals.

Bible Z❂NE

Animal Antics

Say: Jesus was born in a stable, a place for animals. Mary wrapped the baby in soft cloths and laid him in a manger. A manger is a feeding box for animals. Let's pretend to be the animals at the manger.

Encourage the children to wear their animal headbands (**Reproducible 1B**) and pretend to be the animals at the manger. Sing "The Animal Song" to the tune of "The Farmer in the Dell." Have the children move as suggested in the song. End the movements in your story area.

The animals were in the stable;
The animals were in the stable.
On that special Christmas night
The animals were in the stable.

The donkey walked like this;
The donkey walked like this.
On that special Christmas night
The donkey walked like this.

The cow walked like this;
The cow walked like this.
On that special Christmas night
The cow walked like this.

The sheep walked like this;
The sheep walked like this.
On that special Christmas night
The sheep walked like this.

The dove flew like this;
The dove flew like this.
On that special Christmas night
The dove flew like this.

The animals saw the baby;
The animals saw the baby.
On that special Christmas night
The animals saw the baby.

Supplies:
headbands
(Reproducible 1B)

Zillies®:
none

Sign 'n Say

Teach the children the Bible verse, "A child is born to us!" (Isaiah 9:6, *Good News Bible*), in American Sign Language.

© 1998 Abingdon Press

Supplies:
none

Zillies®:
none

Child—Place arms like holding a baby.

Born—Put the back of the right hand in the left palm. Move both hands forward and up.

Us—Touch your right shoulder with your index finger. Circle the finger out and touch it to your left shoulder.

In the Stable

by Daphna Flegal

Encourage the children to wear their animal headbands **(Reproducible 1B)** and to join you in the story area. Tell the children the story in a quiet voice. Have the children make the animal sounds with you.

Baa, baa. Baa, baa. The soft wooly sheep curled up on the hay.

Moo, moo. Moo, moo. The big brown cow closed her eyes.

Hee haw, hee haw. Hee haw, hee haw. The little grey donkey lay down.

Coo, coo. Coo, coo. The small gentle dove tucked his head under his wing.

It was nighttime. It was time for the animals to sleep in the stable.

Then something happened! A man and a woman came into the stable. It was Joseph and Mary. They had traveled a long way to get to Bethlehem. They were very tired, and it was time for Mary's baby to be born. Joseph made a bed for Mary in the soft hay.

Baa, baa. Baa, baa. The soft wooly sheep stood up.

Moo, moo. Moo, moo. The big brown cow opened her eyes.

Hee haw, hee haw. Hee haw, hee haw. The little grey donkey stood up.

Coo, coo. Coo, coo. The small gentle dove raised his head.

Waa, waa. Waa, waa. Baby Jesus was born in the stable that night. Mary wrapped baby Jesus in soft cloths. Joseph filled the manger with hay. Mary laid baby Jesus in the manger.

Baa, baa. Baa, baa. The soft wooly sheep looked in the manger.

Moo, moo. Moo, moo. The big brown cow sniffed at the manger.

Hee haw, hee haw. Hee haw, hee haw. The little grey donkey knelt next to the manger.

Coo, coo. Coo, coo. The small gentle dove flew down to sit on the side of the manger.

Mary sang a lullaby to baby Jesus.

Baa, baa. Baa, baa. The soft wooly sheep curled up on the hay.

Moo, moo. Moo, moo. The big brown cow closed her eyes.

Hee haw, hee haw. Hee haw, hee haw. The little grey donkey lay down.

Coo, coo. Coo, coo. The small gentle dove tucked his head under his wing.

Soon baby Jesus and the animals were fast asleep.

Bible Verse Buzz

Choose a child to hold the Bible open to Isaiah 9:6.

Say: Today our Bible story is about when Jesus was born.

Say the Bible verse, "A child is born to us!" (Isaiah 9:6, *Good News Bible*), for the children. Have the children say the Bible verse after you.

Turn your back to the children or hide your hands underneath a table or behind the **BibleZone® FUNspirational® Kit** lid as you place the **BZ Bee puppet** (see page 174) on your hand. Turn around or bring the puppet out where the children can see it.

Pretend to make the puppet talk. Change your voice for the puppet:

Bzzz. Bzzz. Bzzz. Hi, everybody! I'm BZ Bee. *Bzzz. Bzzz. Bzzz.* I like to taste fingers. Do you have fingers? Yum, yum, yum. Let me taste.

Go to each child. Encourage, but do not force, each child to hold up his or her fingers. Have BZ pretend to taste each child's fingers. Have BZ say things like:

Mmmm. Mmmm. You taste like honey.
Bzzz. Bzzz. You taste like strawberries.
Yumm. Yumm. You taste like blueberries.

After BZ has tasted each child's fingers, say:

Bzzz. Bzzz. Bzzz. I like to taste your fingers. They're yummy. (*Rub BZ's stomach*).

Bzzz. Bzzz. Bzzz. I like something else even more than fingers.

I like the Bible. *Bzzz. Bzzz. Bzzz.* You heard a Bible story today. Who was the baby in the story? (*Jesus*) Where was baby Jesus born? (*in a stable*)

Bzzz. Bzzz. Bzzz. Jesus was born to show God's love.

> ## We praise and thank God for Jesus.

Bzzz. Bzzz. Bzzz. Let's all say the Bible verse together.

"A child is born to us!" (Isaiah 9:6, *Good News Bible*).

Have the children repeat the Bible verse with BZ Bee.

Have BZ Bee say goodbye to the children. Put the puppet away.

Bible Zone

Choose one or more activities to immerse your children in the Bible story.

Supplies:
tambourines
(Reproducible 1A),
cassette player

Zillies®:
Cassette

Sing!

Have the children bring their tambourines **(Reproducible 1A)** and move to an open area of the room.

Say: Today our Bible story is about when baby Jesus was born. Jesus was born to show God's love.

ZONE IN | **We praise and thank God for Jesus.**

Play "An African Nativity" from the **Cassette**. Encourage the children to dance and to wave their tambourines to the music.

An African Nativity
(Sing Noel)

Sing Noel, sing Noel: Noel, noel;
Sing Noel, sing Noel: Noel, noel.
Sing Noel, sing Noel: Noel, noel;
Sing Noel, sing Noel: Noel, noel.

Sing we all Noel, sing we all Noel;
Sing we all Noel, sing we all Noel.
Sing we all Noel, sing we all Noel;
Sing we all Noel, sing we all Noel.

Sing Noel, sing Noel: Noel, noel;
Sing Noel, sing Noel: Noel, noel.
Sing Noel, sing Noel: Noel, noel;
Sing Noel, sing Noel: Noel, noel.
Sing. Sing. Sing.

Life ⓩ⦿ℕℰ

Choose one or more activities to bring the Bible to life.

Star Freeze

Supplies:
headbands
(Reproducible 1B)

Zillies®:
celestial ball

Let the children wear their animal headbands **(Reproducible 1B)** and move to an open area in the room. Show the children the **celestial ball.**

Say: Jesus was born in a stable, a place for animals. When baby Jesus was born, a star appeared in the sky. Let's pretend to be the animals in the stable. Move around the room as if you were one of the animals. When I hold the star ball up above my head, freeze in place. When everyone is frozen, we will all shout, Thank you, God, for baby Jesus!"

Encourage the children to pretend to be animals. After a few minutes hold up the star ball. Have the children freeze in place and then shout, "Thank you, God, for baby Jesus!" Repeat the game several times.

Star Games

Supplies:
none

Zillies®:
celestial ball

Have the children stand in a line. Show the children the **celestial ball.**

Say: When baby Jesus was born, a star appeared in the sky. Pass the ball over your heads as if it were a star shining in the sky.

Encourage the children to pass the celestial ball over their heads. Take the ball from the last child in line.

Say: Now let's pretend the star is twirling around in the sky. Pass the ball down the line. When you get the ball, turn around one time and then pass the ball to the next person.

Give the ball to the first child in the line. Have the child hold the ball and turn around one time. Then have the child pass the ball to the next child.

Say: Now let's pass the ball and say the Bible verse, "A child is born to us!" (Isaiah 9:6, *Good News Bible*).

Give the first child in line the ball. Have the child hold the ball over his or her head, say the Bible verse, and pass the ball to the next child. Continue until each child has held the ball and said the Bible verse.

Say: We praise and thank God for Jesus.

Supplies:
none

Zillies®:
none

Stable Song

Have the children sit in a circle on the floor.

Sing the song printed below to the tune of "Little Cabin in the Woods." Do the suggested motions with the children.

Little stable in the town,
(Make a tent overhead with the hands, fingertips touching.)
Bright starlight is shining down.
(Hold both hands up, fingers outstretched.
Wiggle fingers as you bring the arms down.)
Tiny baby, God's own Son,
(Pretend to rock a baby.)
Jesus is the One.
(Touch palm of left hand with middle finger of right hand;
touch palm of right hand with middle finger of left hand.
Then hold up index finger of right hand, indicating number one.)

Supplies:
none

Zillies®:
camel beanbag

Caravan Prayers

Have the children sit in a circle on the floor. Show the children the **camel beanbag** .

Say: Jesus was born in a stable, a place for animals. There might have been a camel in the stable when Jesus was born. Let's pretend the camel is walking around our circle.

Say the following poem as the children pass the camel beanbag around the circle.

Harump, harump,
The camel walks this way,
As we thank God for Jesus,
Born on Christmas Day.

Pray: Thank you, God, for baby Jesus. Thank you for (*name each child*).
Amen.

Photocopy the **HomeZone®** newsletter to send home to parents.

In the Stable

Today's Bible story centers around the birth of Jesus. Mary and Joseph had to travel to Bethlehem before Jesus was born. After a long, dusty journey they arrived in the crowded city. Instead of being able to get a room in the inn, Joseph and Mary ended up with animals in a stable. It was here that Jesus was born.

It does not seem possible that God's Son would be born in a place for animals, but God constantly surprises us with impossible things. Let your child enjoy God's surprises as he or she learns the Christmas story.

Bible Verse
A child is born to us!
Isaiah 9:6, Good News Bible

Bible Story
Luke 2:1–7

Stable Song

Sing the song printed below to the tune of "Little Cabin in the Woods." Do the suggested motions with your child.

Little stable in the town,
(Make a tent overhead with the hands, fingertips touching.)
Bright starlight is shining down.
(Hold both hands up, fingers outstretched. Wiggle fingers as you bring the arms down.)
Tiny baby, God's own Son,
(Pretend to be rocking a baby.)
Jesus is the One.
(Touch palm of left hand with middle finger of right hand; touch palm of right hand with middle finger of left hand. Then hold up index finger of right hand, indicating number one.)

We praise and thank God for Jesus.

19

Reproducible 1A

BIBLEZONE®

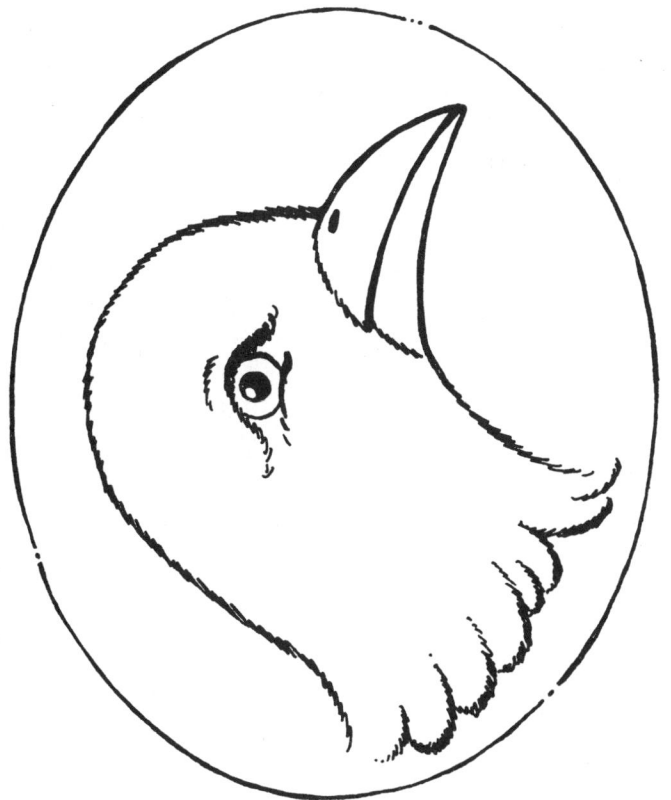

Reproducible 1B

By the Star's Light

Enter the Z⦿NE®

Bible Verse
A child is born to us!
Isaiah 9:6, *Good News Bible*

Bible Story
Matthew 2:1–12

A star is the symbol of Epiphany, a commemoration of the visit of the magi to Jesus. The only place where this story is told in the Bible is in the Book of Matthew.

Many believe that the kings of the Matthew story were astrologers, and therefore it was not unusual for them to be scanning the heavens looking for signs of great events. For such astrologers following a star would be natural.

We are not told how many wise men there were on this journey. Tradition assumes there were three of them because there were three gifts. Frankincense was a perfume used in the holy oils that anointed priests, and it was also used in incense. Myrrh was an aromatic tree gum used in perfumes and for embalming. And gold was valuable for the same reasons it's considered valuable today. It was the presentation of these gifts to the Christ child that has been the inspiration for gift giving at Christmas.

The wise men did not arrive in Bethlehem until Jesus was probably around two years old. This is probably why Herod ordered the death of all male Jewish children up to two years old.

When the wise men found the child, they knelt down and worshiped him—not the normal reaction when visiting a child, but appropriate when visiting the King of kings.

Herod wanted the wise men to betray the child to him. However, they were warned by an angel and did not return to Herod. They went home another way.

ZONE IN

We praise and thank God for Jesus.

Scope the ZONE

ZONE	TIME	SUPPLIES	⊚ ZILLIES®
Zoom Into the Zone			
Stardots	10 minutes	Reproducible 2A, tape	prism star stickers
Wise Waistcoats	10 minutes	grocery-size paper bags, scissors; fabric, ribbon, or lace scraps, glue; glitter crayons	prism star stickers
BibleZone®			
Follow the Footprints	10 minutes	Reproducible 2B, tape, scissors	none
The Very Special Star	10 minutes	two AA batteries	star glitter wand
Bible Verse Buzz	5 minutes	Bible, BZ Bee	none
Sing!	5 minutes	cassette player, two AA batteries	Cassette, star glitter wand
LifeZone			
Glitter 'n Glaze	10 minutes	Reproducible 2B, scissors, newspapers; Epsom salts, crayons, water, shallow container, spoon, cotton balls; glitter crayons or scented markers; or glitter, cotton swabs, glue, box lid or shallow tray; paper punch, yarn	none
Gift Exchange	10 minutes	none	none
Star Walk	5 minutes	basket or box	celestial ball
Caravan Prayers	5 minutes	none	camel beanbag

⊚ Zillies® are found in the **BibleZone® FUNspirational® Kit.**

Zoom Into the *Zone*

Choose one or more activities to catch your children's interest.

Supplies:
Reproducible 2A,
tape

Zillies®:
prims star stickers

Stardots

Photocopy the dot-to-dot star for each child **(Reproducible 2A)**. Give the children prism star stickers. Encourage each child to place a star sticker over each dot on his or her star. Tape the stars around the room.

Say: **When Jesus was born, a star appeared in the sky. Wise men followed the star to find Jesus. The journey took the wise men a long time, but they followed the star to Bethlehem. When they saw Jesus, they knelt down and gave him gifts.**

> **We praise and thank God for Jesus.**

Supplies:
grocery-size paper bags; scissors; fabric, ribbon, or lace scraps; glue; glitter crayons

Zillies®:
prism star stickers

Wise Waistcoats

Before class begins, cut a grocery-size paper bag to make a coat for each child. Turn each sack upside down. Cut a slit up the middle of one of the wider sides. At the top of the slit, continue to cut and form a circular shape for the child's neck. Out of each narrow side, cut a hole large enough for a child's arm to go through. If your bags have printing on them, turn the bags inside out.

Give each child a paper bag. Encourage the children to decorate the paper bags to be robes like the wise men might have worn. Let the children use **prism star stickers**. The children might also glue on scraps of fabric, ribbon, and lace. Or let the children decorate the bags with glitter crayons. Encourage the children to wear the coats for the rest of the lesson.

Say: **When Jesus was born, a star appeared in the sky. Wise men followed the star to find Jesus. The journey took the wise men a long time, but they followed the star to Bethlehem. When they saw Jesus, they knelt down and gave him gifts.**

> **We praise and thank God for Jesus.**

Bible ZONE®

Choose one or more activities to immerse your children in the Bible story.

Follow the Footprints

Supplies:
Reproducible 2B,
tape, scissors

Zillies®:
none

Make several photocopies of the camel footprints and the star **(Reproducible 2B)**. Use the footprints to make a winding path around your room. Place several stars along the footprint path at various intervals. Secure the footprints and stars with tape.

Say: When Jesus was born, a star appeared in the sky. Wise men followed the star to find Jesus. The journey took the wise men a long time, but they followed the star to Bethlehem. Let's follow the camel footprints and say our Bible verse to praise and thank God for Jesus.

ZONE IN®

> **We praise and thank God for Jesus.**

Have the children line up at the beginning of the path. Encourage the children to follow the camel footprints around the room. Each time the children come to a star, have the children stop and sign the Bible verse, "A child is born to us!" (Isaiah 9:6, *Good News Bible*).

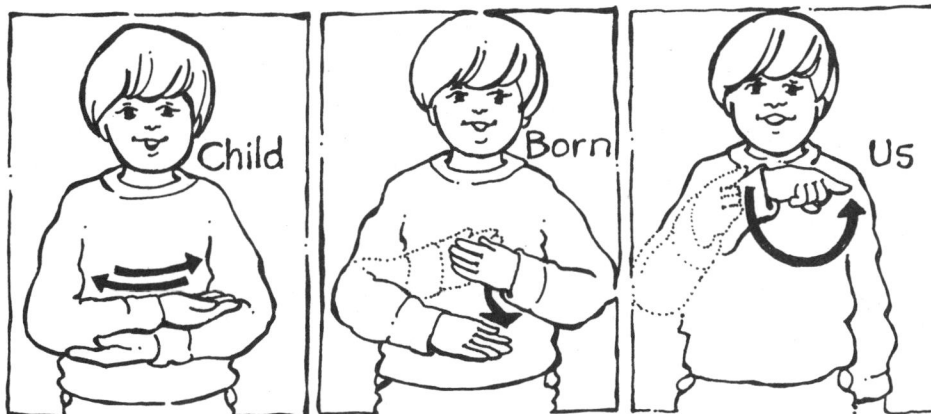

Child | Born | Us

© 1998 Abingdon Press

Child—Place arms like holding a baby.

Born—Put the back of the right hand in the palm of the left hand. Move both hands forward and up.

Us—Touch your right shoulder with your index finger. Circle the finger out and then touch the finger to your left shoulder.

The Very Special Star

by Daphna Flegal

*Invite the children to sit down in your story area. Show the children the **star glitter wand**.*

Say: Watch me as I tell the Bible story. Each time I hold up the star, say, "Sparkle, sparkle."

Practice holding up the star and saying the words with the children.

Some wise men lived in a country far, far away. Every night they looked at the sky. They were searching for a very special **star**.

(Hold up the star glitter wand.)
Sparkle, sparkle.

They wanted to find the baby born to be king. They knew they could find the king by following the very special **star**.

(Hold up the star glitter wand.)
Sparkle, sparkle.

One night the wise men saw a light sparkling in the sky. The light sparkled bigger and brighter than all the other lights. They knew they had found the very special **star**.

(Hold up the star glitter wand.)
Sparkle, sparkle.

The wise men quickly prepared for a long journey. They packed food and water. They packed blankets and clothes. They packed treasure chests with gifts for the king. Then the wise men began their journey led by the very special **star**.

(Hold up the star glitter wand.)
Sparkle, sparkle.

It was a long journey. The wise men traveled night after night, always following the bright light of the very special **star**.

(Hold up the star glitter wand.)
Sparkle, sparkle.

Finally the bright light stopped in a little town named Bethlehem. The wise men saw a house underneath the light of the very special **star**.

(Hold up the star glitter wand.)
Sparkle, sparkle.

The wise men went inside the house. They found Mary and Jesus! Jesus was the king! The wise men knelt down. They opened their treasure chests and gave Jesus their gifts. They were very happy that they had followed the very special **star**.

(Hold up the star glitter wand.)
Sparkle, sparkle.

Bible Verse Buzz

Choose a child to hold the Bible open to Isaiah 9:6.

Say: Today our Bible story is about when the wise men followed the star to find Jesus.

Say the Bible verse, "A child is born to us!" (Isaiah 9:6, *Good News Bible*), for the children. Have the children say the Bible verse after you.

Turn your back to the children or hide your hands underneath a table or behind the **BibleZone® FUNspirational® Kit** lid as you place the **BZ Bee puppet** (see page 174) on your hand. Turn around or bring the puppet out where the children can see it.

Pretend to make the puppet talk. Change your voice for the puppet:

Bzzz. Bzzz. Bzzz. Hi, everybody! I'm BZ Bee. *Bzzz. Bzzz. Bzzz.* I like to taste fingers. Do you have fingers? Yum, yum, yum. Let me taste.

Go to each child. Encourage, but do not force, each child to hold up his or her fingers. Have BZ pretend to taste each child's fingers. Have BZ say things like:

Mmmm. Mmmm. You taste like honey. *Bzzz. Bzzz.* You taste like strawberries. *Yumm. Yumm.* You taste like blueberries.

After BZ has tasted each child's fingers, say:

Bzzz. Bzzz. Bzzz. I like to taste your fingers. They're yummy. *(Rub BZ's stomach).*

Bzzz. Bzzz. Bzzz. I like something else even more than fingers.

I like the Bible. *Bzzz. Bzzz. Bzzz.* You heard a Bible story today. What were the wise men looking for in the sky? *(a star)* Where did the wise men go? *(to find Jesus.)*

Bzzz. Bzzz. Bzzz. The wise men followed the star to find Jesus.

> **Zone In**
>
> **We praise and thank God for Jesus.**

Bzzz. Bzzz. Bzzz. Let's all say the Bible verse together.

"A child is born to us!" (Isaiah 9:6, *Good News Bible*).

Have the children repeat the Bible verse with BZ Bee.

Have BZ Bee say goodbye to the children. Put the puppet away.

Choose one or more activities to immerse your children in the Bible story.

Supplies:
cassette player, two AA batteries

Zillies®:
Cassette, star glitter wand

Sing!

Have the children line up behind you. Hold the **star glitter wand** in your hand.

Say: Today our Bible story is about when the wise men followed the star to find Jesus.

> **ZONE IN**
> **We praise and thank God for Jesus.**

Play "An African Nativity" from the **Cassette.** Hold up the glitter wand and lead the children around the room as the music plays.

An African Nativity
(Sing Noel)

Sing Noel, sing Noel: Noel, noel;
Sing Noel, sing Noel: Noel, noel.
Sing Noel, sing Noel: Noel, noel;
Sing Noel, sing Noel: Noel, noel.

Sing we all Noel, sing we all Noel;
Sing we all Noel, sing we all Noel.
Sing we all Noel, sing we all Noel;
Sing we all Noel, sing we all Noel.

Sing Noel, sing Noel: Noel, noel;
Sing Noel, sing Noel: Noel, noel.
Sing Noel, sing Noel: Noel, noel;
Sing Noel, sing Noel: Noel, noel.
Sing. Sing. Sing.

Glitter 'n Glaze

(P) hotocopy and cut out the star **(Reproducible 2B)** for each child. Cover the tables with newspaper.

Let the children decorate the stars in one of the following ways:

Epsom salts. Have the children decorate the stars with crayons. Mix equal parts of Epsom salts and water in a shallow container. Stir until the salt dissolves. Show the children how to dip a cotton ball into the mixture and then rub the mixture over the stars. The water will evaporate and crystals will appear.

Glitter crayons or scented markers. Let the children decorate the stars with glitter crayons or with scented markers.

Glitter. Have the children use cotton swabs to spread glue over the stars. Place each star in a box lid or a shallow tray. Show the children how to shake glitter over the glue. Shake off the excess glitter into a trash container.

Use a paper punch to punch a hole in the top of each star. Tie a loop of yarn through the hole to make a hanger.

Say: When Jesus was born, a star appeared in the sky. Wise men followed the star to find Jesus.

Supplies:
Reproducible 2B, newspaper, scissors, Epsom salts, water, crayons, shallow container, spoon, cotton balls; glitter crayons or scented markers; or glitter, cotton swabs, glue, box lid or shallow tray; paper punch, yarn

Zillies®:
none

Gift Exchange

(S) ay: The wise men gave Jesus three gifts. The gifts were gold, frankincense, and myrrh. *(Have the children repeat the names of the gifts.)* **Let's pretend to be the three gifts.**

Have the children stand in a circle. Go around the circle and say the name of one of the gifts for each child. Have that child repeat the name. Explain that each child needs to remember the name of his or her gift.

Say: Gold and frankincense change places.

All the children who named gold and frankincense should change places. Continue the game, calling out the names of the gifts and having the children change places. Sometimes call only one name; sometimes call all three.

Supplies:
none

Zillies®:
none

Supplies:
basket or box

Zillies®:
celestial ball

Star Walk

Place a basket or box on one side of the room. Set the **celestial ball** in the basket or box. Have the children line up on the opposite side of the room. Choose the first child in line to begin the game.

Say: *(Child's name)*, **you walk like a camel to the star.**

Have the child walk like a camel across the room to the star. Then have the child pick up the star ball, hold it above his or her head, say the Bible verse, "A child is born to us!" (Isaiah 9:6, *Good News Bible*), and replace the ball in the box. Continue the game until each child has had a turn moving to the ball. Use the following suggestions for how to have the children move:

Pretend you are an angel flying to the star.
Move like you are a comet shooting across the sky to the star.
Pretend you are a cloud floating to the star.

Supplies:
none

Zillies®:
camel beanbag

Caravan Prayers

Have the children sit in a circle on the floor. Show the children the **camel beanbag** .

Say: **The wise men followed the star to find Jesus. The wise men may have ridden camels on their long journey following the star. Let's pretend the camel is walking around our circle.**

Say the following poem as the children pass the camel beanbag around the circle.

Harump, harump,
The camel walks this way,
As we thank God for Jesus,
Born on Christmas Day.

Pray: **Thank you, God, for baby Jesus. Thank you for** *(name each child)* **Amen..**

Photocopy the **HomeZone®** newsletter to send home to parents.

Home Zone For Parents

By the Star's Light

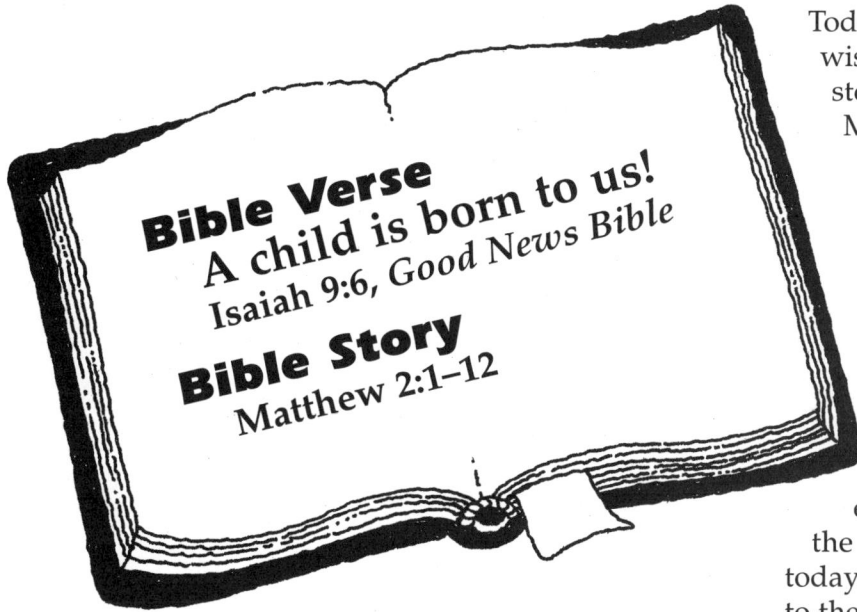

Today your child heard the story of the wise men. The only place where this story is told in the Bible is in the Book of Matthew.

We were not told how many wise men there were on this journey. Tradition assumes there were three of them because there were three gifts. Frankincense was a perfume used in the holy oils that anointed priests, and it was also used in incense. Myrrh was an aromatic tree gum used in perfumes and for embalming. And gold was valuable for the same reasons it's considered valuable today. It was the presentation of these gifts to the Christ child that has been the inspiration for gift giving at Christmas.

The wise men did not arrive in Bethlehem until Jesus was probably around two years old. When the wise men found the child, they knelt down and worshiped him—not the normal reaction when visiting a child, but appropriate when visiting the King of kings.

Bible Verse
A child is born to us!
Isaiah 9:6, *Good News Bible*

Bible Story
Matthew 2:1–12

Sign 'n Say

Teach the children the Bible verse, "A child is born to us!" (Isaiah 9:6, *Good News Bible*), in American Sign Language.

Child—Place arms like holding a baby.

Born—Put the back of the right hand in the palm of the left hand. Move both hands forward and up.

Us—Touch your right shoulder with your index finger. Circle the finger out and then touch the finger to your left shoulder.

Child | Born | Us

© 1998 Abingdon Press

We praise and thank God for Jesus.

Permission granted to photocopy for local church use. © 1999 Abingdon Press.

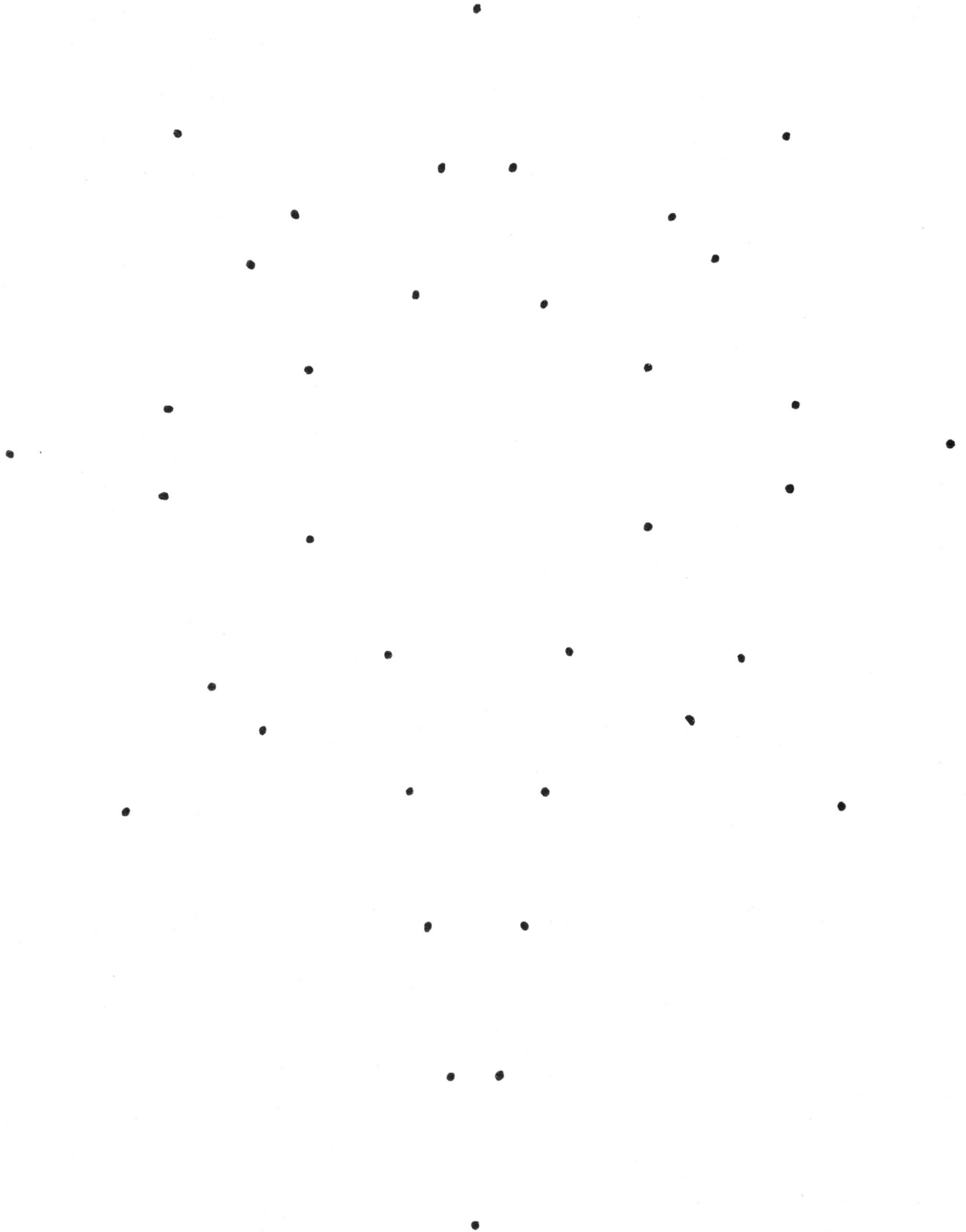

Reproducible 2A

Permission granted to photocopy for local church use. © 1999 Abingdon Press.

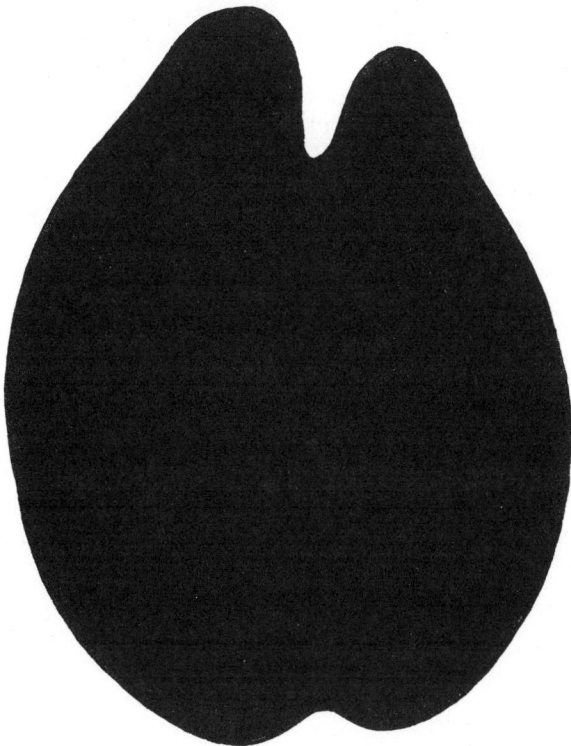

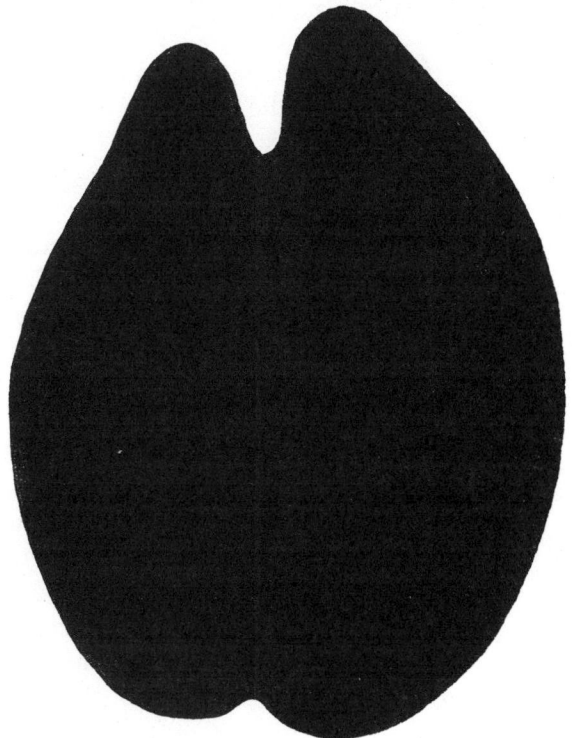

Reproducible 2B

With the Elders

Enter the Zone

Bible Verse
Jesus grew both in body and in wisdom.
Luke 2:52, *Good News Bible*

Bible Story
Luke 2:39–52

These verses in Luke are the only references to Jesus between the time of his infancy and the time that he started his ministry. What do they tell us?

Mary and Joseph were devout Jews, so we can assume that he received the normal Jewish upbringing. Jesus would have attended the synagogue and learned the Scriptures of the Old Testament. Three times every year he would have gone with his family (or at least with Joseph) to the annual festivals prescribed for male Israelites. Women were not required to attend, but frequently did. The Passover celebration was particularly important. Jesus would have attended these festivals many times before he was twelve.

When Jesus was found in the Temple, he was "sitting among the teachers, listening to them and asking them questions" (Luke 2:46). In one of the halls of the Temple's outer courts, the rabbis used question, answer, and discussion to teach. Jesus' interest in learning and religion is evident by his attendance at one of these sessions.

Was Jesus aware at this time of his special relationship with God? Luke seems to think he was.

However, Jesus was obedient to his earthly parents and returned home with them, where he "grew and became strong, filled with wisdom; and the favor of God was upon him" (Luke 2:40). Already, years before his ministry began, the preparation for that ministry had started.

Young children often have trouble understanding that the baby Jesus born at Christmas is the man named Jesus. We can help them begin to understand this concept by teaching them about Jesus' childhood and growth.

We grow and learn about God.

Scope the ZONE

ZONE	TIME	SUPPLIES	⊚ ZILLIES®
Zoom Into the Zone			
Temple Tint	5 minutes	Reproducible 3A; gold or yellow crayons, markers, or glitter crayons	none
Temple Two Step	10 minutes	Reproducible 3B, scissors, tape	none
BibleZone®			
Wonder Works	5 minutes	none	none
Sign 'n Say	5 minutes	none	none
A Long Walk	10 minutes	none	none
Bible Verse Buzz	5 minutes	Bible, BZ Bee	none
Sing!	5 minutes	cassette player	Cassette
LifeZone			
Where Is Jesus?	10 minutes	none	smile face beanbag key chain
Learning Limbo	10 minutes	two chairs, scissors	ribbon
Bible Verse Sing-along	5 minutes	none	none
Caravan Prayers	5 minutes	none	camel beanbag

⊚ Zillies® are found in the **BibleZone® FUNspirational® Kit.**

Choose one or more activities to catch your children's interest.

Supplies:
Reproducible 3A;
gold or yellow
crayons, markers, or
glitter crayons

Zillies®:
none

Temple Tint

(P) hotocopy the picture of the Temple (**Reproducible 3A**) for each child.

Say: **Jesus grew just like we grow. He grew from a baby to a boy to a man. Today our story is about when Jesus was a boy. When Jesus was twelve years old, he went to the Temple with his family. The Temple was a special place to worship God. It was a beautiful place made of gold and stone. Let's add gold to our Temples.**

Let the children color the Temples with gold or yellow crayons, markers, or glitter crayons. Read the Bible verse printed on the pictures to the children. Display the pictures in your story area.

Say: **As Jesus grew, he learned about God.**

We grow and learn about God.

Supplies:
Reproducible 3B,
tape, scissors

Zillies®:
none

Temple Two Step

(P) hotocopy and cut apart several copies of the footprints (**Reproducible 3B**). Make a path on the floor with the footprints. Use a loop of tape on the back of each footprint to secure the footprint to the floor. Wind the footprint path around your room and end the path in your story area, where you have displayed the Temple pictures.

Say: **Jesus grew just like we grow. He grew from a baby to a boy to a man. Today our story is about when Jesus was a boy. When Jesus was twelve years old, he went to the Temple with his family. Let's pretend to go to the Temple. We will follow the path of footprints along the floor. Each one of you will get to be the leader.**

Have the children line up one behind the other. Choose the first child in line to be the leader. Have the child lead the children in walking along the footprint path to the Temple. Then have the children go back to the beginning of the path. Choose a different leader. Have that child lead the children in crawling along the footprint path to the Temple. Continue that game until each child has had a turn being the leader. Change the movement with each leader (tiptoe, march, hop, walk backwards, and so forth).

Bible Zone

Choose one or more activities to immerse your children in the Bible story.

Wonder Works

Supplies:
none

Zillies®:
none

Have the children stand in your story area. Lead the children in the following movement activity.

Jesus grew from a baby,
(Rock baby in your arms.)
Just like me and you.
(Point to self; point to others.)
And when he grew into a boy,
(Crouch down, then stand up tall.)
I wonder what he could do?
(Put finger on the side of your head.)

I wonder if Jesus could . . .
jump! Let's all jump.
I wonder if Jesus could . . .
run! Let's all run in place.
I wonder if Jesus could . . .
hop! Let's all hop on one foot.
I wonder if Jesus could . . .
sit! Let's all sit down.

Say: As Jesus grew, he learned about God.

ZONE IN

We grow and learn about God.

Sign 'n Say

Supplies:
none

Zillies®:
none

Teach the children the Bible verse, "Jesus grew both in body and in wisdom" (Luke 2:52, *Good News Bible*), in American Sign Language.

Jesus—Touch the middle finger of the right hand to the palm of the left hand. Reverse.

Grew—Let the thumb and fingers of the left hand form an open circle, with the palm facing right. Push the right open hand up through the left hand.

Body—Touch your chest with both open palms. Repeat the motion slightly lower on body.

Wisdom—Bend the index finger of the right hand. Move the bent finger up and down in front of the forehead.

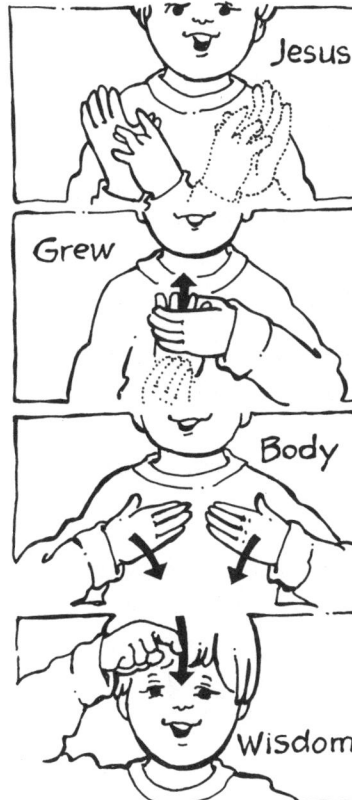

Jesus

Grew

Body

Wisdom

© 1998 Abingdon Press

A Long Walk

by Daphna Flegal

Have the children sit in a circle on the floor.

Say: Our Bible story today is about when Jesus was a boy. Jesus and his family walked to the Temple. When I tell about the walk in the story, we will pat our legs to make the sound of footsteps.

Show the children how to pat their legs in a steady rhythm. Tell the children the story and do the suggested motions.

When Jesus was a boy, he went with his family to the Temple, a special place to worship God.

It was a long walk to the Temple. *(Pat legs in a steady rhythm.)* Jesus and his family walked and walked. They walked with their friends. They walked with other people in their family.

Finally they got to the Temple. *(Stop patting legs.)* It was a beautiful place.

(Point to eyes.) Jesus saw many, many people. *(Point to nose.)* Jesus smelled the fire burning at the altar. *(Point to ears.)* Jesus heard the teachers at the Temple talk about God.

Soon it was time to go. Mary and Joseph began the long walk home. *(Pat legs in a steady rhythm.)* They walked for one whole day. Then they stopped. *(Stop patting legs.)* Jesus was not with them!

Mary and Joseph looked for Jesus among their friends. But Jesus was not there! *(Shake head no.)* They looked for Jesus among their family. But Jesus was not there! *(Shake head no.)*

Mary and Joseph hurried back to the Temple. *(Pat legs quickly.)* Jesus was there! *(Stop patting legs; shake head yes.)*

Jesus was listening to the teachers talk about God. *(Point to ears.)* He was asking the teachers questions about God.

"What are you doing?" Mary asked Jesus. "Joseph and I have been looking all over for you. We were worried."

"I thought you would know I was here at the Temple," Jesus said to Mary. "I want to learn more about God."

Jesus and his family started the long walk home. *(Pat legs in a steady rhythm.)* As they walked together, Mary thought about how much she loved Jesus.

Bible Verse Buzz

Choose a child to hold the Bible open to Luke 2:52.

Say: Today our Bible story is about when Jesus was a boy.

Say the Bible verse, "Jesus grew both in body and in wisdom" (Luke 2:52, *Good News Bible*), for the children. Have the children say the Bible verse after you.

Turn your back to the children or hide your hands underneath a table or behind the **BibleZone® FUNspirational® Kit** lid as you place the **BZ Bee puppet** (see page 174) on your hand. Turn around or bring the puppet out where the children can see it.

Pretend to make the puppet talk. Change your voice for the puppet:

Bzzz. Bzzz. Bzzz. Hi, everybody! I'm BZ Bee. *Bzzz. Bzzz. Bzzz.* I like to taste fingers. Do you have fingers? Yum, yum, yum. Let me taste.

Go to each child. Encourage, but do not force, each child to hold up his or her fingers. Have BZ pretend to taste each child's fingers. Have BZ say things like:

Mmmm. Mmmm. You taste like honey. *Bzzz. Bzzz.* You taste like strawberries. *Yumm. Yumm.* You taste like blueberries.

After BZ has tasted each child's fingers, say:

Bzzz. Bzzz. Bzzz. I like to taste your fingers. They're yummy. *(Rub BZ's stomach).*

Bzzz. Bzzz. Bzzz. I like something else even more than fingers.

I like the Bible. *Bzzz. Bzzz. Bzzz.* You heard a Bible story today. Who was the boy in the story? *(Jesus)* Where did Jesus go with his family? *(to the Temple)*

Bzzz. Bzzz. Bzzz. As Jesus grew, he learned about God.

Zone IN	**We grow and learn about God.**

Bzzz. Bzzz. Bzzz. Let's all say the Bible verse together.

"Jesus grew both in body and in wisdom" (Luke 2:52, *Good News Bible*).

Have the children repeat the Bible verse with BZ Bee.

Have BZ Bee say goodbye to the children. Put the puppet away.

Bible Z⌀NE

Choose one or more activities to immerse your children in the Bible story.

Supplies:
cassette player

Zillies®:
Cassette

Sing!

Have the children stand in a circle. Play the song "Jesus in the Morning" from the **Cassette**. Do the suggested motions with the children as the music plays.

Jesus in the Morning

(Have the children hold hands and walk around the circle.)
Jesus, Jesus,
Jesus in the morning,
Jesus at the noontime;
Jesus, Jesus,
Jesus when the sun goes down.
(Have the children drop hands and squat down to touch the floor.)

(Have the children put their hands over their hearts.)
Love Him, love Him,
love Him in the morning,
love Him at the noontime;
love Him, love Him,
love Him when the sun goes down.
(Have the children drop hands and squat down to touch the floor.)

(Have the children hold hands out, palms up.)
Serve Him, serve Him,
serve Him in the morning,
serve Him at the noontime;
serve Him, serve Him,
serve Him when the sun goes down.
(Have the children drop hands and squat down to touch the floor.)

(Have the children hold hands and walk around the circle.)
Jesus, Jesus,
Jesus in the morning,
Jesus at the noontime.
Jesus, Jesus,
Jesus when the sun goes down.
Jesus when the sun goes down.
Jesus when the sun goes down.
(Have the children drop hands and squat down to touch the floor.)

Where Is Jesus?

Supplies:
none

Zillies®:
smile face beanbag
key chain

Have the children sit in a circle on the floor.

Say: **Today our story is about when Jesus was a boy. When Jesus was twelve years old, he went to the Temple with his family. When Mary and Joseph started home, they did not know that Jesus was missing. Let's help Mary and Joseph find Jesus.**

Show the children the **smile face beanbag key chain**. Explain to the children that the beanbag will be a pretend Jesus. Choose one child to be "it." Have "it" cover his or her eyes or go out of the room with a teacher. Hide the smile face beanbag somewhere in the room. Make sure the remaining children know where you place the beanbag. Have "it" uncover his or her eyes or come back into the room.

Say: **(Child's name), where is Jesus?**

Have "it" look around the room to find Jesus. When "it" moves close to Jesus, have the other children say, "You're hot." When "it" moves away from Jesus, have the other children say, "You're cold." When "it" finds Jesus, clap for the child and have everyone repeat the Bible verse, "Jesus grew both in body and in wisdom" (Luke 2:52, *Good News Bible*).

Learning Limbo

Supplies:
two chairs, scissors

Zillies®:
ribbon

Place two chairs opposite each other in an open area of the room. Tie a length of **ribbon** (about four feet) between the two chairs. Have the children sit down on the floor, facing the ribbon.

Say: **As Jesus grew, he learned about God. Let's think about what we have learned about God.**

Give the children the following directions. Have the children move back and forth underneath the ribbon as suggested.

If you have learned that God loves you, crawl under the ribbon. (*Have all the children crawl under the ribbon.*) **If you have learned that God is always with you, slide under the ribbon.** (*Have all the children slide on their stomachs under the ribbon.*) **If you have learned that you can talk to God anytime or anywhere, roll under the ribbon.** (*Have the children lie down on the floor and roll under the ribbon.*)

Life Zone

Choose one or more activities to bring the Bible to life.

Supplies:
none

Zillies®:
none

Bible Verse Sing-along

Have the children sit in a circle on the floor.

Say: Jesus grew just like we grow. He grew from a baby to a boy to a man. As Jesus grew, he learned about God.

Sing the Bible verse with the children. The tune is "Hot Cross Buns."

Jesus grew.
Jesus grew.
Both in body and in wisdom,
Jesus grew.

Supplies:
none

Zillies®:
camel beanbag

Caravan Prayers

Have the children sit in a circle on the floor. Show the children the **camel beanbag** .

Say: Jesus grew from a baby to a boy. When Jesus was a boy, he went with his family to the Temple. Jesus and his family walked a long way to go to the Temple. Let's pretend the camel is walking around our circle.

Say the following poem as the children pass the camel beanbag around the circle.

Harump, harump,
The camel walks this way,
As we thank God for Jesus,
Born on Christmas Day.

Pray: Thank you, God, for the boy, Jesus. Thank you for *(name each child)*. Amen.

Photocopy the **HomeZone®** newsletter to send home to parents.

42

BIBLEZONE®

Home Zone For Parents

With the Elders

Today your child heard the story of when Jesus went to the Temple as a boy. These verses in Luke are the only references to Jesus between the time of his infancy and the time that he started his ministry. They tell us that Jesus learned about God as he grew.

Young children often have trouble understanding that the baby Jesus born at Christmas is the man named Jesus. We can help them begin to understand this concept by teaching them about Jesus' childhood and growth.

Bible Verse
Jesus grew both in body and in wisdom.
Luke 2:52, *Good News Bible*

Bible Story
Luke 2:39–52

Sign 'n Say

Learn the Bible verse, "Jesus grew both in body and in wisdom" (Luke 2:52, *Good News Bible*), in American Sign Language.

Jesus—Touch the middle finger of the right hand to the palm of the left hand. Reverse.

Grew—Let the thumb and fingers of the left hand form an open circle, with the palm facing right. Push the right open hand up through the left hand.

Body—Touch your chest with both open palms. Repeat the motion slightly lower on the body.

Wisdom—Bend the index finger of the right hand. Move the bent finger up and down in front of the forehead.

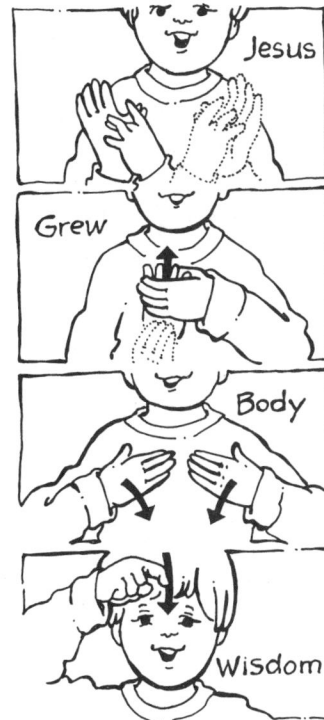

© 1998 Abingdon Press

We grow and learn about God.

Permission granted to photocopy for local church use. © 1999 Abingdon Press.

43

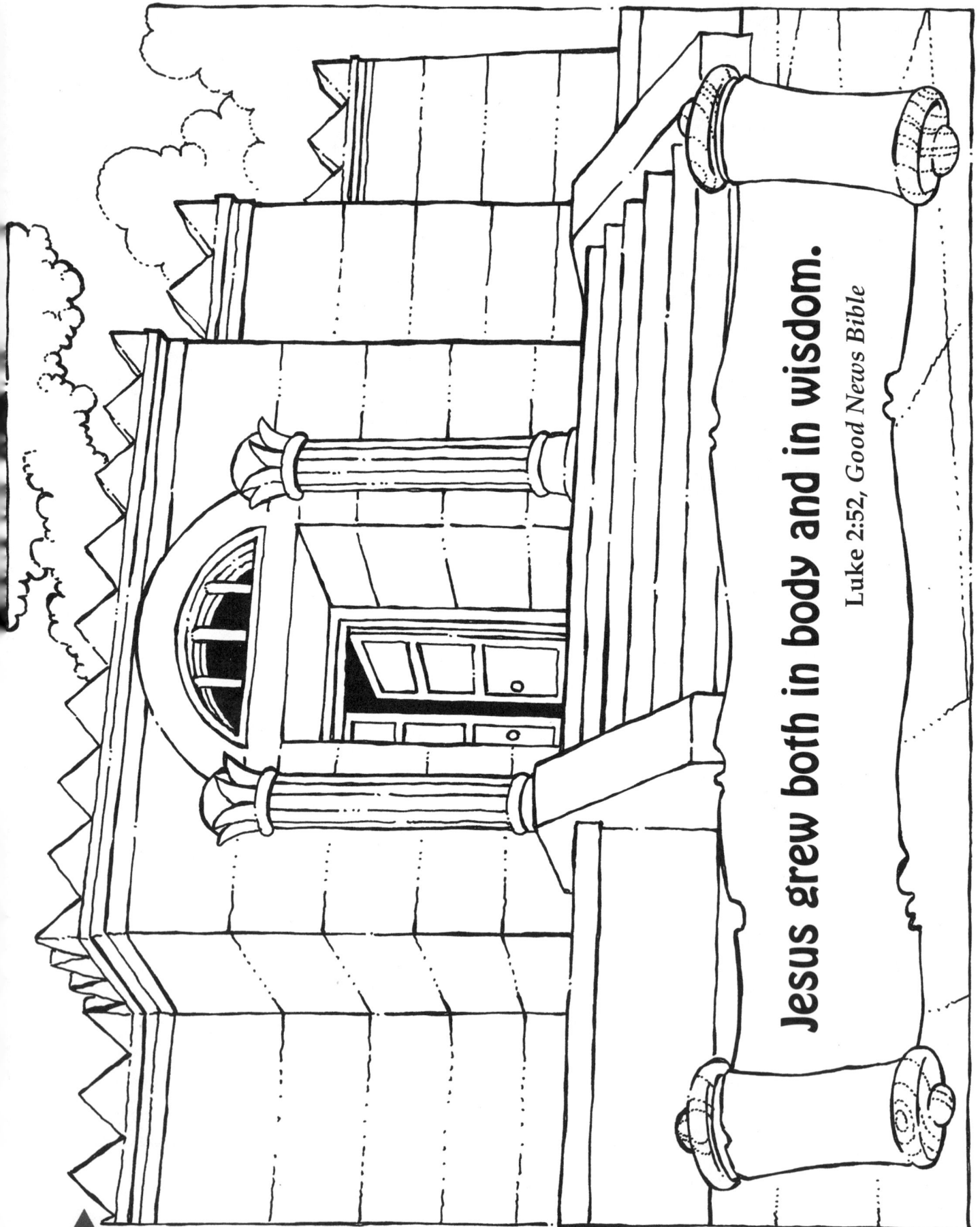

Jesus grew both in body and in wisdom.

Luke 2:52, *Good News Bible*

Reproducible 3A

BIBLEZONE®

Reproducible 3B

At the River

Enter the ZONE

Bible Verse
Jesus grew both in body and in wisdom.

Luke 2:52, *Good News Bible*

Bible Story
Luke 3:15–23

John, the son of Elizabeth and Zechariah, and the cousin of Jesus, grew up to be a preacher. John called the people to repent in preparation for the coming of the kingdom of God. John would then baptize people.

Baptism did not start with John the Baptist. It had long been practiced by Jews as a rite of religious purification to receive new converts into the Jewish faith. Gentiles wanting to convert to Judaism were baptized to cleanse themselves of non-Jewish beliefs and practices.

The baptism John practiced was different in that it was a rite of repentance so that sins could be forgiven. Repentance meant a complete change of will and behavior. Baptism was (and is) an outward sign of an inward change. The ritual of baptism also marks a person as a member of the family of God.

Why did Jesus seek baptism from John? We do not believe it was because of any sin. Luke uses the baptism as the time when the sign was given that Jesus was God's Son. Even John the Baptist at first objected to baptizing Jesus (Matthew 3:14-15). Jesus'

response to John's objections shows that Jesus endorsed John's ministry and that his baptism was an act of obedience to God's will for all people. This would be consistent with Jesus' whole ministry, which showed people through actions as well as words what obedience to God meant.

Whatever the reason for his baptism, it marked the beginning of Jesus' own ministry and is still used as the sign of our relationship with God.

The Bible tells us that when Jesus was baptized, the heavens opened and a dove came down to Jesus. Then a voice spoke, saying, "You are my Son, the Beloved; with you I am well pleased" (Luke 3:22).

Jesus is God's Son.

Scope the Zone

ZONE	TIME	SUPPLIES	ZILLIES®
Zoom Into the Zone			
Water Power	10 minutes	plastic, dishpan, water, plastic containers	turkey basters
Water Waves	15 minutes	Reproducible 4A, dishpan, water, crayons or markers, tape safety scissors, paper punch, yarn	none
BibleZone®			
Wonder Works	5 minutes	none	none
Sign 'n Say	5 minutes	none	none
Jesus Is God's Son	10 minutes	water waves (Reproducible 4A)	none
Bible Verse Buzz	5 minutes	Bible, BZ Bee	none
Sing!	5 minutes	water waves (Reproducible 4A), cassette player	Cassette
LifeZone			
Fine Feathers	10 minutes	Reproducible 4B, newspaper, paint smocks, paper towels, shallow container, white tempera paint, hand-washing supplies	none
Fly Away	10 minutes	none	none
Bible Verse Sing-along	5 minutes	none	none
Pillow Prayers	5 minutes	none	inflatable feather pillow

Zillies® are found in the **BibleZone® FUNspirational® Kit.**

Zoom Into the ZONE

Choose one or more activities to catch your children's interest.

Supplies:

plastic, dishpan, water, plastic containers

Zillies®:

turkey basters

Water Power

Cover the table with plastic. Place a dishpan partially filled with water on the table. Float empty plastic containers on the water. Set out the **turkey basters**. Show the children how to fill a turkey baster with water from the dishpan and then to squirt the water on the containers. Let the children try to make the containers sink.

Say: **Jesus grew from a baby to a boy to a man. Today our Bible story is about when Jesus was a man. Jesus was baptized with water from a river. As Jesus was baptized, a dove flew down from the sky, and a voice spoke. The voice told Jesus that God loved him and that he was God's Son.**

Jesus is God's Son.

Supplies:

Reproducible 4A, dishpan, water, crayons or markers, tape, safety scissors, paper punch, yarn

Zillies®:

Water Waves

Photocopy the water waves page **(Reproducible 4A)** for each child. Use the dishpan you partially filled with water from the "Water Power" activity. Let the children watch as you swirl the water with a finger. Give each child a water waves page. Encourage the children to use crayons or markers to make water swirls on the top part (with the printed Bible verse) of the waves.

When the children have finished coloring, tape each wave to the table so that the solid horizontal line is along the edge of the table. This will leave the bottom two-thirds of the page hanging over the edge of the table. Show each child how to cut the solid vertical lines up to the edge of the table. These strips will make the streamer part of the water waves.

Use a paper punch to punch two holes in the top of each water wave. Tie a loop of yarn through the holes to make a handle. Show the children how to hold the handles and wave their water waves.

Say: **Today our Bible story is about when Jesus was baptized with water from a river. Let's pretend our papers are waves in the water.**

Write each child's name on her or his water wave. Place the water waves in your story area.

Bible ZONE

Choose one or more activities to immerse your children in the Bible story.

Wonder Works

Supplies:
none

Zillies®:
none

(H) ave the children stand in your story area. Lead the children in the following movement activity.

Jesus grew from a baby,
(Rock baby in your arms.)
Just like me and you.
(Point to self; point to others.)
And when he grew into a boy,
(Crouch down, then stand up tall.)
I wonder what he could do?
(Put finger on the side of your head.)

I wonder if Jesus could . . .
    jump! Let's all jump.
I wonder if Jesus could . . .
    run! Let's all run in place.
I wonder if Jesus could . . .
    hop! Let's all hop on one foot.
I wonder if Jesus could . . .
    sit! Let's all sit down.

Say: Jesus grew from a baby to a boy to a man. When Jesus was a man, he was baptized. He saw a dove and heard a voice say that he was God's Son.

ZONE IN

Jesus is God's Son.

Sign 'n Say

Supplies:
none

Zillies®:
none

(T) each the Bible verse, "Jesus grew both in body and in wisdom" (Luke 2:52, *Good News Bible*), in American Sign Language.

Jesus—Touch the middle finger of the right hand to the palm of the left hand. Reverse.

Grew—Let the thumb and fingers of the left hand form an open circle, with the palm facing right. Push the right open hand up through the left hand.

Body—Touch your chest with both open palms. Repeat the motion slightly lower on the body.

Wisdom—Bend the index finger of the right hand. Move the bent finger up and down in front of the forehead.

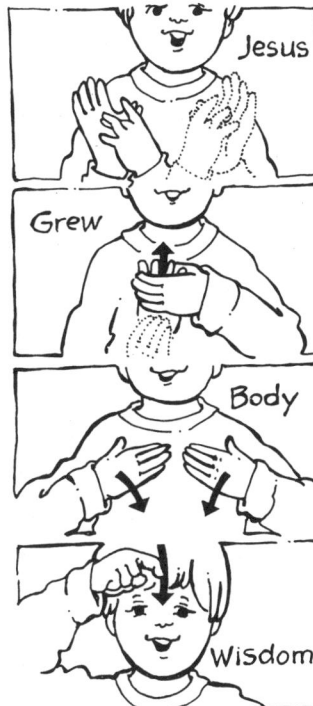

Jesus

Grew

Body

Wisdom

© 1998 Abingdon Press

Jesus Is God's Son

by Daphna Flegal

Have the children bring their water waves **(Reproducible 4A)** and sit down in your story area.

Say: I want you to help me tell the Bible story today. Each time I say, "God's Son," I want you to wave your water waves and say, "Jesus is God's Son."

Have the children practice.

"Come," the man called to the people. "Come to the water. Come and hear good news."

The man was John the Baptist. He talked to people by the side of the river. He told people the good news about **God's Son.**

Jesus is God's Son. *(Have the children wave the water waves and repeat the words.)*

"Come into the water," said John. "Tell God you are sorry for the wrong things you have done. Let me baptize you."

Many people came to the river to be baptized by John. Many people heard John tell the good news about **God's Son.**

Jesus is God's Son. *(Have the children wave the water waves and repeat the words.)*

One day Jesus came to the river. He watched as John baptized people in the water of the Jordan River. He listened as John told people the good news about **God's Son.**

Jesus is God's Son. *(Have the children wave the water waves and repeat the words.)*

"I want you to baptize me," Jesus said to John. Jesus walked into the water of the Jordan River. John baptized Jesus with the water. John knew that Jesus was **God's Son.**

Jesus is God's Son. *(Have the children wave the water waves and repeat the words.)*

As Jesus came out of the river, he saw a dove flying down from the sky. Jesus heard God's voice. "You are my Son, the Beloved; with you I am pleased." Jesus knew that he was **God's Son.**

Jesus is God's Son. *(Have the children wave the water waves and repeat the words.)*

Jesus is God's Son. *(Have the children wave the water waves and repeat the words.)*

Jesus is God's Son. *(Have the children wave the water waves and repeat the words.)*

Adapted from "God's Own Dear Son"
Touch the Water, Taste the Bread, Ages 3-5 © 1998 by Cokesbury.

Bible Verse Buzz

Choose a child to hold the Bible open to Luke 2:52.

Say: Jesus grew from a baby to a boy to a man. Today our Bible story is about when Jesus was a man. Jesus was baptized with water from a river.

Say the Bible verse, "Jesus grew both in body and in wisdom" (Luke 2:52, *Good News Bible*), for the children. Have the children say the Bible verse after you.

Turn your back to the children or hide your hands underneath a table or behind the **BibleZone® FUNspirational® Kit** lid as you place the **BZ Bee puppet** (see page 174) on your hand. Turn around or bring the puppet out where the children can see it.

Pretend to make the puppet talk. Change your voice for the puppet:

Bzzz. Bzzz. Bzzz. Hi, everybody! I'm BZ Bee. *Bzzz. Bzzz. Bzzz.* I like to taste fingers. Do you have fingers? Yum, yum, yum. Let me taste.

Go to each child. Encourage, but do not force, each child to hold up his or her fingers. Have BZ pretend to taste each child's fingers. Have BZ say things like:

Mmmm. Mmmm. You taste like honey. *Bzzz. Bzzz.* You taste like strawberries. *Yumm. Yumm.* You taste like blueberries.

After BZ has tasted each child's fingers, say:

Bzzz. Bzzz. Bzzz. I like to taste your fingers. They're yummy. *(Rub BZ's stomach).*

Bzzz. Bzzz. Bzzz. I like something else even more than fingers.

I like the Bible. *Bzzz. Bzzz. Bzzz.* You heard a Bible story today. Who was the man in the story? *(Jesus)* Where was Jesus baptized? *(in a river)* What did Jesus see? *(a dove)*

Bzzz. Bzzz. Bzzz. As Jesus was baptized, a dove flew down from the sky, and a voice spoke. The voice told Jesus that God loved him and that he was God's Son.

Jesus is God's Son.

Bzzz. Bzzz. Bzzz. Let's all say the Bible verse together.

"Jesus grew both in body and in wisdom" (Luke 2:52, *Good News Bible*).

Have the children repeat the Bible verse with BZ Bee.

Have BZ Bee say goodbye to the children.

Bible Z⊙NE

Choose one or more activities to immerse your children in the Bible story.

Supplies:
water waves
(Reproducible 4A),
cassette player

Zillies®:
Cassette

Sing!

Have the children bring their water waves **(Reproducible 4A)** and move to an open area of the room. Play the song, "Do You Know the Son of God?" from the **Cassette.** Let the children dance and wave their water waves as the music plays.

Do You Know the Son of God?

The Son of God,
The Son of God?
Do you know the Son of God
Who died and rose again?

Yes, I know the Son of God,
The Son of God,
The Son of God.
Yes, I know the Son of God
Who died and rose again.

Jesus is the Son of God,
The Son of God,
The Son of God.
Jesus is the Son of God
Who died and rose again.

Writers: Ruth Schram and Ed Kee

From the Brentwood-Benson Music Publishing, Inc., recording, *Mother Goose Gospel, Vol. 1.*

Life Zone

Fine Feathers

(P) hotocopy the dove picture **(Reproducible 4B)** for each child. Give each child a picture.

Cover the table with newspaper and have the children wear paint smocks. Fold paper towels and place them in the bottom of a shallow container. Pour white tempera paint onto the paper towels to make a paint pad.

Show the children how to press their thumbs onto the paint pad and then onto their doves to make thumbprints. The prints will make the feathers for the doves. Set the pictures flat to dry. Have the children wash their hands.

Say: **Jesus grew from a baby to a boy to a man. Today our Bible story is about when Jesus was a man. Jesus was baptized with water from a river. As Jesus was baptized, a dove flew down from the sky, and a voice spoke. The voice told Jesus that God loved him and that he was God's Son.**

Jesus is God's Son.

Supplies:
Reproducible 4B, newspaper, paint smocks, paper towels, shallow container, white tempera paint, hand-washing supplies

Zillies®:
none

Fly Away

(H) ave the children sit down in a circle in an open area of the room.

Say: **As Jesus was baptized, a dove flew down from the sky, and a voice spoke. The voice told Jesus that God loved him and that he was God's Son. Let's take turns pretending to be the dove.**

Choose one child to be the dove. Have the dove fly around the outside of the circle as you say the following rhyme. When you say, "Fly back home, *(child's name)*," have the child sit back down. Repeat the rhyme and let each child have a turn flying around the circle as the dove.

> See the dove flying in the sky.
> Flying, flying up so high.
> Flying down from up above.
> To tell us all about God's love.
> Fly back home, *(child's name)*.
> God loves you.

Supplies:
none

Zillies®:

Choose one or more activities to bring the Bible to life.

Supplies:
none

Zillies®:
none

Bible Verse Sing-along

Have the children sit in a circle on the floor.

Say: **Jesus grew just like we grow. He grew from a baby to a boy to a man. As Jesus grew, he learned about God.**

Sing the Bible verse with the children. The tune is "Hot Cross Buns."

> Jesus grew.
> Jesus grew.
> Both in body and in wisdom,
> Jesus grew.

Supplies:
none

Zillies®:
inflatable feather pillow

Pillow Prayers

Have the children sit in a circle on the floor.

Say: **Jesus grew from a baby to a boy to a man. When Jesus was a man, he was baptized with water from a river. As Jesus was baptized, a dove flew down from the sky, and a voice spoke. The voice told Jesus that God loved him and that he was God's Son.**

Show the children the **inflatable feather pillow.**

Say: **The feathers in our pillow can remind us about the dove. We can remember that Jesus is God's Son.**

Pass the pillow around the circle. As each child holds the pillow, have the child **say, "Jesus is God's Son."**

Pray: **Thank you, God, for loving** (*name each child*). **Amen.**

Photocopy the **HomeZone**® newsletter to send home to parents.

At the River

Today your child heard the Bible story of when Jesus was baptized by John. The Bible tells us that when Jesus was baptized, the heavens opened, and a dove came down to Jesus. Then a voice spoke, saying "You are my Son, the Beloved; with you I am well pleased" (Luke 3:22). Jesus' baptism showed that he belonged to God and that God was with him. It also marked the beginning of his ministry.

Remind your child that we all belong to God. God loves each of us.

Bible Verse
Jesus grew both in body and in wisdom.
Luke 2:52, *Good News Bible*

Bible Story
Luke 3:15–23

Watercolors

Let your child paint with watercolors. Or give your child a piece of plain paper. Encourage your child to draw with watercolor markers on the paper. Partially fill the sink with water. As soon as your child finishes coloring, dip the paper into the sink. The water will make the colors run and give the picture a watery effect. Set the picture flat to dry.

Remind your child that Jesus was baptized with water. When Jesus was baptized, he saw a dove in the sky and heard a voice telling him that God loved him and that he was God's Son.

ZONE IN

Jesus is God's Son.

Jesus grew both in body and in wisdom.
Luke 2:52, Good News Bible

Reproducible 4A

BibleZone®

Reproducible 4B

Permission granted to photocopy for local church use. © 1999 Abingdon Press.

In the Desert

Enter the Z@NE

Bible Verse
Jesus grew both in body and in wisdom.
Luke 2:52, *Good News Bible*

Bible Story
Luke 4:1–13; Matthew 4:1–11; Mark 1:12–13

After Jesus was baptized, he was led by the Holy Spirit into the wilderness or desert, and there began a struggle.

A call to ministry or vocation often causes a struggle between the call and worldly considerations. The beginning of Jesus' ministry was marked by a particularly dramatic struggle.

Many biblical scholars agree that Jesus' experience in the wilderness was a time in which Jesus struggled to establish a direction for his ministry. In the Gospel of Luke the temptations Jesus faced were defined as temptations to turn from the ministry of God.

The three temptations Jesus faced in this encounter in the wilderness were repeated in various forms throughout his ministry. The temptations to work a miracle to satisfy an immediate need (food), to give a miraculous sign of who he was (the Messiah), and to exercise political power in this world showed up in other forms as Jesus' ministry was lived out.

Jesus never swayed from his determination to fulfill his ministry. Jesus' ministry was defined by his refusal to give into these

temptations. People's needs are spiritual as well as physical. Political power is not the power that God had sent him to exercise. And by not giving into the temptation of testing God by throwing himself from the pinnacle of the Temple, Jesus placed his ministry above that of mere magic. Jesus always remained faithful to the will of God.

The emphasis of this lesson for preschool children is on the Bible. Jesus used the Scriptures to help him turn away from the temptations and do what God wanted him to do. We can teach young children that the Bible is a special book that helps us learn what God wants us to do.

The Bible helps us know what God wants us to do.

Scope the ZONE

ZONE	TIME	SUPPLIES	⊚ ZILLIES®
Zoom Into the Zone			
Desert Sands	10 minutes	Reproducible 5A, tape, crayons with papers removed	sandpaper
Wonderful Words	10 minutes	Reproducible 5B, crayons or markers	none
BibleZone®			
Wonder Works	5 minutes	none	none
Sign 'n Say	5 minutes	none	none
Bible Words	10 minutes	Bible storybooks (Reproducible 5B)	none
Bible Verse Buzz	5 minutes	Bible, BZ Bee	none
Sing!	5 minutes	cassette player	Cassette
LifeZone			
Work Out	10 minutes	none	none
Bible Verse Sing-along	5 minutes	none	none
Pillow Prayers	5 minutes	none	inflatable feather pillow

⊚ Zillies® are found in the **BibleZone® FUNspirational® Kit.**

Zoom Into the Zone

Supplies:
Reproducible 5A, tape, crayons with papers removed

Zillies®:
sandpaper

Desert Sands

(P) hotocopy the the picture of Jesus in the desert **(Reproducible 5A)** for each child. Tape **sandpaper** to the table in front of each child. Help the children lightly tape their pictures over the sandpaper. Show the children how to use the sides of the crayons to color over the sandpaper. The texture will show through on their pictures.

Say: **Jesus grew from a baby to a boy to a man. When Jesus was a man, he went to the desert. Our picture shows Jesus in the desert. While Jesus was there, he was tempted to do things God did not want him to do. But Jesus remembered words from the Bible. The Bible helped him do the things God wanted him to do.**

ZONE IN | **The Bible helps us know what God wants us to do.**

Supplies:
Reproducible 5B, crayons or markers

Zillies®:
none

Wonderful Words

(P) hotocopy the Bible storybook pages **(Reproducible 5B)** for each child. Show the children how to fold the storybooks like greeting cards.

Say: **When Jesus was a man, he went to the desert. While Jesus was there, he was tempted to do things God did not want him to do. But Jesus remembered words from the Bible. The Bible helped him do the things God wanted him to do.**

ZONE IN | **The Bible helps us know what God wants us to do.**

Have the children turn the pages of their Bible storybooks. Read each Bible verse to the children and let the children decorate the pages with crayons or markers.

Write each child's name on her or his storybook. Plan to use the storybooks as you tell today's story.

Choose one or more activities to immerse your children in the Bible story.

Wonder Works

Supplies:
none

Zillies®:
none

(H)ave the children stand in your story area. Lead the children in the following movement activity.

Jesus grew from a baby,
(Rock baby in your arms.)
Just like me and you.
(Point to self; point to others.)
And when he grew into a boy,
(Crouch down, then stand up tall.)
I wonder what he could do?
(Put finger on the side of your head.)

I wonder if Jesus could . . .
　jump! Let's all jump.
I wonder if Jesus could . . .
　run! Let's all run in place.
I wonder if Jesus could . . .
　hop! Let's all hop on one foot.
I wonder if Jesus could . . .
　sit! Let's all sit down.

Say: Jesus grew from a baby to a boy to a man. When Jesus was a man, he went into the wilderness. He was tempted to do things God did not want him to do. But Jesus remembered words from the Bible. The Bible helped him do the things God wanted him to do.

Sign 'n Say

Supplies:
none

Zillies®:
none

(T)each the children the Bible verse, "Jesus grew both in body and in wisdom" (Luke 2:52, *Good News Bible*), in American Sign Language.

Jesus—Touch the middle finger of the right hand to the palm of the left hand. Reverse.

Grew—Let the thumb and fingers of the left hand form an open circle, with the palm facing right. Push the right open hand up through the left hand.

Body—Touch your chest with both open palms. Repeat the motion slightly lower on the body.

Wisdom—Bend the index finger of the right hand. Move the bent finger up and down in front of the forehead.

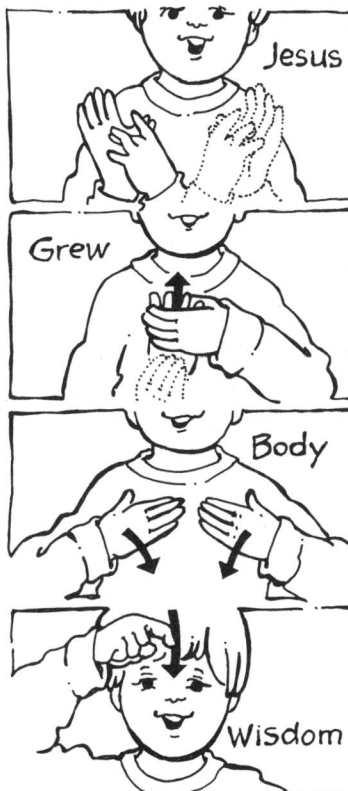

Jesus

Grew

Body

Wisdom

© 1998 Abingdon Press

Bible Words

by Daphna Flegal

*ave the children bring their Bible storybooks (**Reproducible 5B**) and join you in the story area.*

Jesus went to the desert to think about what God wanted him to do. He stayed there for many, many days.

While he was there, he was tempted to do things that God did not want him to do.

But each time Jesus was tempted, he remembered words from the Scriptures. The words helped him do want God wanted him to do. The words helped him choose to serve God.

Our Bible has words that can help us choose to serve God and do what God wants us to do. Let's remember some words from the Bible.

(Have the children open their Bible storybooks to Page 2.)

God is love (1 John 4:8). Now say the Bible verse with me. **God is love** (1 John 4:8). Now let's sing this Bible verse.

*(Sing the song to the tune of "The Wheels on the Bus." Have the children put their palms together to make an open book on the word **Bible**. Have them put their hands over their hearts each time you sing the word **love**.)*

> The Bible tells us God is love,
> God is love, God is love.
> The Bible tells us God is love.
> Let's share God's love.

(Have the children open their Bible storybooks to Page 3.)

Be happy and glad (Matthew 5:12, *Good News Bible*). Now say the Bible verse with me. **Be happy and glad** (Matthew 5:12, *Good News Bible*). Now let's learn this Bible verse with a song.

*(Sing the song to the tune of "The Wheels on the Bus." Have the children put their palms together to make an open book on the word **Bible**. Have them point to their smiles each time you sing the word **glad**.)*

> The Bible tells us, be happy and glad,
> Happy and glad, happy and glad.
> The Bible tells us, be happy and glad.
> Be happy and be glad.

(Have the children open their Bible storybooks to Page 4.)

Pray at all times (Romans 12:12, *Good News Bible*). Now say the Bible verse with me. **Pray at all times** (Romans 12:12, *Good News Bible*). Now let's sing this Bible verse.

*(Sing the song to the tune of "The Wheels on the Bus." Have the children put their palms together to make an open book on the word **Bible**. Have them fold their hands in prayer each time you sing the word **pray**.)*

> The Bible tells us to pray at all times,
> Pray at all times, pray at all times.
> The Bible tells us to pray at all times.
> Pray at all times.

Bible Verse Buzz

Choose a child to hold the Bible open to Luke 2:52.

Say: Jesus grew from a baby to a boy to a man. Today our Bible story is about when Jesus was a man. Jesus went to the desert.

Say the Bible verse, "Jesus grew both in body and in wisdom" (Luke 2:52, *Good News Bible*), for the children. Have the children say the Bible verse after you.

Turn your back to the children or hide your hands underneath a table or behind the **BibleZone® FUNspirational® Kit** lid as you place the **BZ Bee puppet** (see page 174) on your hand. Turn around or bring the puppet out where the children can see it.

Pretend to make the puppet talk. Change your voice for the puppet:

Bzzz. Bzzz. Bzzz. Hi, everybody! I'm BZ Bee. *Bzzz. Bzzz. Bzzz.* I like to taste fingers. Do you have fingers? Yum, yum, yum. Let me taste.

Go to each child. Encourage, but do not force, each child to hold up his or her fingers. Have BZ pretend to taste each child's fingers. Have BZ say things like:

Mmmm. Mmmm. You taste like honey. *Bzzz. Bzzz.* You taste like strawberries. *Yumm. Yumm.* You taste like blueberries.

After BZ has tasted each child's fingers, say:

Bzzz. Bzzz. Bzzz. I like to taste your fingers. They're yummy. *(Rub BZ's stomach.)*

Bzzz. Bzzz. Bzzz. I like something else even more than fingers.

I like the Bible. *Bzzz. Bzzz. Bzzz.* You heard a Bible story today. Who was the man in the story? *(Jesus)* Where did Jesus go in today's story? *(to the desert)* What did Jesus remember when he was tempted in the desert? *(words from the Scriptures or Bible)*

Bzzz. Bzzz. Bzzz. While Jesus was there, he was tempted to do things God did not want him to do. But Jesus remembered words from the Bible. The Bible helped him do the things God wanted him to do.

The Bible helps us know what God wants us to do.

Bzzz. Bzzz. Bzzz. Let's all say the Bible verse together.

"Jesus grew both in body and in wisdom" (Luke 2:52, *Good News Bible*).

Have the children repeat the Bible verse with BZ Bee.

Have BZ Bee say goodbye to the children. Put the puppet away.

Choose one or more activities to immerse your children in the Bible story.

Supplies:
cassette player

Zillies®:
Cassette

Sing!

(P) lay the song, "Do You Know the Son of God?" from the **Cassette.** Let the children sing the song with the Cassette.

Do You Know the Son of God?

The Son of God,
The Son of God?
Do you know the Son of God
Who died and rose again?

Yes, I know the Son of God,
The Son of God,
The Son of God,
Yes, I know the Son of God
Who died and rose again.

Jesus is the Son of God,
The Son of God,
The Son of God.
Jesus is the Son of God
Who died and rose again.

Writers: Ruth Schram and Ed Kee

© 1988 New Spring Publishing, Inc. (ASCAP) (a div. of Brentwood-Benson Music Publishing, Inc.)
All Rights Reserved. Used by Permission.

From the Brentwood-Benson Music Publishing, Inc., recording, *Mother Goose Gospel, Vol. 1.*

Life Zone

Work Out

Have the children move to an open area of the room.

Say: When Jesus was a man, he went to the desert. While Jesus was there, he was tempted to do things God did not want him to do. But Jesus remembered words from the Bible. The Bible helped him do the things God wanted him to do. Let's use our bodies to think about some of the things God wants us to do.

Have the children follow the directions suggested below.

Let's think about our hands. *(Wiggle your hands.)* **Clap your hands.** *(Have the children clap their hands.)* **Wiggle your hands up high**. *(Have the children raise their hands above their heads.)* **Wiggle your hands down low.** *(Have the children wiggle their hands near the floor.)* **How can we use our hands to do what God wants us to do?** *(Let the children respond.)* **If we can use our hands to help others, clap your hands.** *(Have the children clap their hands.)*

Let's think about our feet. *(Wiggle your feet.)* **Stomp your feet.** *(Have the children stomp their feet.)* **Stand on your tiptoes.** *(Have the children stand on their tiptoes.)* **March in place.** *(Have the children march in place.)* **How can we use our feet to do what God wants us to do?** *(Let the children respond.)* **If we can use our feet to go places and tell others about Jesus, stomp your feet.** *(Have the children stomp their feet.)*

Let's think about our ears. *(Touch your ears.)* **Listen with your ears.** *(Have the children cup their hands around their ears.)* **How can we use our ears to do what God wants us to do?** *(Let the children respond.)* **If we can use our ears to listen to stories from the Bible, touch your ears.** *(Have the children touch their ears.)*

Let's think about our mouths. *(Point to your mouth.)* **Stick out your tongue.** *(Have the children stick out their tongues.)* **Sing "La, la, la."** *(Have the children sing.)* **How can we use our mouths to do what God wants us to do?** *(Let the children respond.)* **If we can use our mouths to praise God, shout "Hurray!"** *(Have the children shout "Hurray!")*

Let's think about our whole bodies. *(Touch your head, your shoulders, your knees, and your toes.)* **If we can use our bodies to do what God wants us to do, jump three times!** *(Have the children jump.)*

Supplies:
none

Zillies®:

Life Zone

Choose one or more activities to bring the Bible to life.

Supplies:
none

Zillies®:
none

Bible Verse Sing-along

Have the children sit in a circle on the floor.

Say: Jesus grew just like we grow. He grew from a baby to a boy to a man. As Jesus grew, he learned about God.

Sing the Bible verse with the children. The tune is "Hot Cross Buns."

> Jesus grew.
> Jesus grew.
> Both in body and in wisdom,
> Jesus grew.

Supplies:
none

Zillies®:
inflatable feather pillow

Pillow Prayers

Have the children sit in a circle on the floor.

Say: Jesus grew from a baby to a boy to a man. When Jesus was a man, he was baptized with water from a river. As Jesus was baptized, a dove flew down from the sky, and a voice spoke. The voice told Jesus that God loved him and that he was God's Son. After Jesus was baptized, he went to the desert. While Jesus was there, he was tempted to do things God did not want him to do. But Jesus remembered words from the Bible. The Bible helped him do the things God wanted him to do.

Show the children the **inflatable feather pillow.**

Say: The feathers in our pillow can remind us about the dove. We can remember that the Bible tells us Jesus is God's Son.

Pass the pillow around the circle. As each child holds the pillow, have the child **say, "Jesus is God's Son."**

Pray: Thank you, God, for loving (name each child). Amen.

Photocopy the **HomeZone®** newsletter to send home to parents.

Bible Verse
Jesus grew both in body and in wisdom.
Luke 2:52, *Good News Bible*

Bible Story
Luke 4:1–13; Matthew 4:1–11;
Mark 1:12–13

In the Desert

After Jesus was baptized, he was led by the Holy Spirit into the wilderness or desert, where he was tempted to turn away from serving God. But with the help of the Scriptures, Jesus made the choice to serve God.

The emphasis of this lesson for preschool children is on the Bible. Jesus used the Scriptures to help him turn away from the temptations and do what God wanted him to do. Teach your child that the Bible is a special book that helps us learn what God wants us to do.

Desert Dessert

Purchase a package of instant butterscotch pudding. Let your child help you make the pudding according to the directions on the package.

Place a few vanilla wafers or graham crackers into a resealable bag. Securely fasten the bag. Let your child smash, shake, and crush the cookies to make cookie crumbs.

Layer the pudding and cookie crumbs into clear plastic cups to make "desert" scenes. Say a thank-you prayer, eat, and enjoy!

Remind your child that when Jesus grew to be a man, he went into the desert. While Jesus was there, he was tempted to do things God did not want him to do. But Jesus remembered words from the Scriptures. The Scriptures helped him do the things God wanted him to do.

ZONE IN
The Bible helps us know what God wants us to do.

Reproducible 5A

Permission granted to photocopy for local church use. © 1999 Abingdon Press.

BibleZone®

Be happy and glad.
Matthew 5:12, Good News Bible

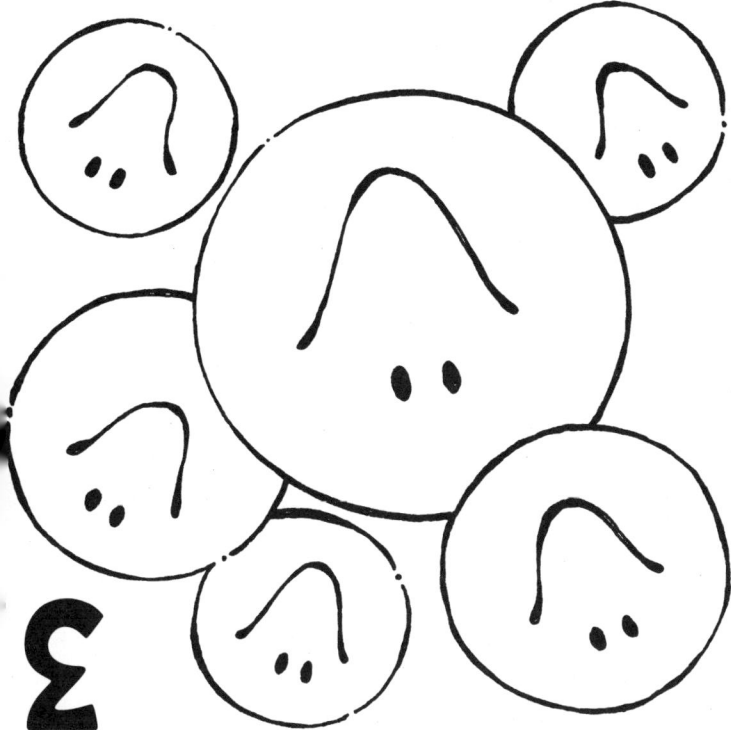

God is love. 1 John 4:8

2

4

Pray at all times.
Romans 12:12, Good News Bible

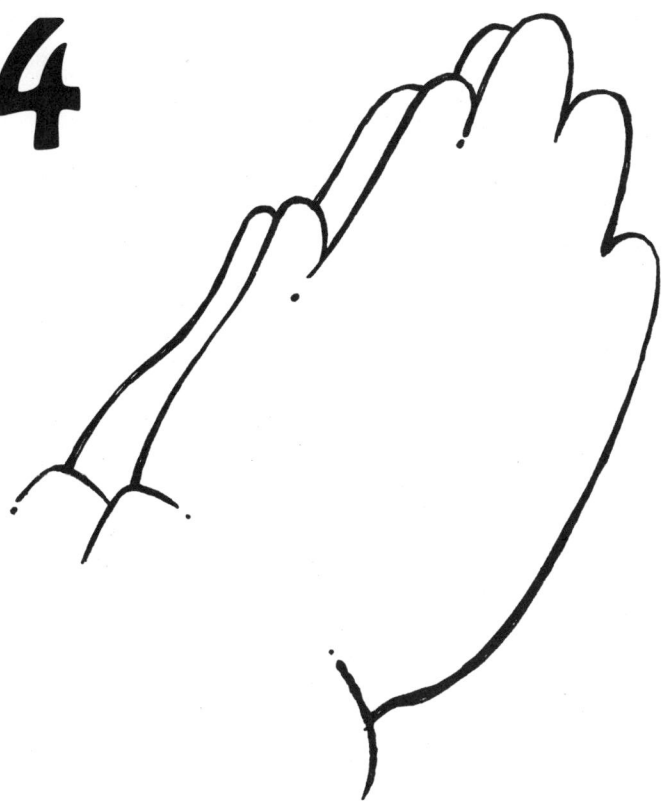

HOLY
BIBLE

1

Reproducible 5B

At the Synagogue

Enter the ZONE

Bible Verse
Jesus grew both in body and in wisdom.
Luke 2:52, *Good News Bible*

Bible Story
Luke 4:16-30; Matthew 13:54-58; Mark 6:1-6

We all know the old saying, "Familiarity breeds contempt." This certainly applies to the opening stages of Jesus' ministry in his hometown of Nazareth.

Here is the carpenter's son, a quite likeable fellow. He comes from good stock, but now he's becoming a little pretentious, a little "big for his britches." Just who does he think he is? What makes him think he understands God better than we do?

The rejection of Jesus' ministry by those who had seen him grow up was not unusual. After all, they thought they knew this man, but what they had seen was merely the man. They had not recognized his special relationship with God.

Jesus had been baptized and then had struggled with Satan in the wilderness. He could not be the same. He was destined for other things. Not having lived through these things with him, the people of Nazareth could not understand this change.

Jesus announced in the synagogue in Nazareth that his ministry would be for the poor and the oppressed. It was a message people were not eager to hear, and they certainly did not want to hear it from this man who was one of them.

In Jesus' announcement he used Scripture to tell the kind of Messiah he would be—he would preach good news, he would help the needy, and he would bring relief to those who were oppressed. While the people in Nazareth rejected this announcement, it is good news for us.

As teachers, we have the responsibility to bring the good news to children. What is the good news for preschool children? The good news is that God loves each one of them.

We can tell others the good news about God's love.

Scope the Zone

ZONE	TIME	SUPPLIES	ZILLIES
Zoom Into the Zone			
Synagogue Setup	5 minutes	small table or large box; masking tape; pillows, carpet samples, benches, or chairs	none
Scrolling Along	10 minutes	Reproducible 6A, rolled paper, scissors, glue, crayons or markers	none
BibleZone®			
Wonder Works	5 minutes	none	none
Sign 'n Say	5 minutes	none	none
Step, Step, Step	10 minutes	Reproducible 6A, scissors	none
Bible Verse Buzz	5 minutes	Bible, BZ Bee	none
Sing!	5 minutes	cassette player	Cassette
LifeZone			
Unroll the Scroll	5 minutes	scrolls (Reproducible 6A)	none
Good News Games	10 minutes	Reproducible 6B, scissors, clear tape, masking tape	none
Bible Verse Sing-along	5 minutes	none	none
Pillow Prayers	5 minutes	none	inflatable feather pillow

Zillies® are found in the **BibleZone® FUNspirational® Kit.**

Zoom Into the Zone

Choose one or more activities to catch your children's interest.

Supplies:
small table or large box; masking tape; pillows, carpet samples, benches, or chairs

Zillies®:
none

Synagogue Setup

Involve the children in setting up an area of your classroom to be a synagogue.

Say: People in Bible times went to the synagogue to worship and to learn about God. The synagogue was an important building. Let's make a pretend synagogue.

Use a small table or a large box to be the place where the scrolls or Scriptures were kept. Use masking tape to outline a large rectangle on the floor in front of the table. Let the children place pillows, carpet samples, benches, or chairs in front of the table.

Say: Jesus grew from a baby to a boy to a man. Today our Bible story is about when Jesus was a man. Jesus went to the synagogue in his hometown. While he was there, he read from the Scriptures. He told the people that God wanted him to tell others the good news about God's love.

> **We can tell others the good news about God's love.**

Supplies:
Reproducible 6A, rolled paper, scissors, glue, crayons or markers

Zillies®:
none

Scrolling Along

Cut a piece of rolled paper about 24 inches long for each child. Photocopy and cut apart the story pictures (**Reproducible 6A**) for each child. Let the children color the pictures with crayons or markers.

Say: Jesus grew from a baby to a boy to a man. Today our Bible story is about when Jesus was a man. Jesus went to Nazareth, his hometown. He went to the synagogue. While he was there, he read from the Scriptures. The Scriptures were written on a scroll. He told the people that God wanted him to tell them the good news about God's love. The people in his hometown did not want to listen to Jesus. Jesus left his hometown and went to tell others the good news about God's love.

Give each child the rolled paper. Let the children glue the pictures onto the papers. Show the children how to roll each end of the paper toward the middle to make scrolls. Write each child's name on the outside of her or his scroll. Have the children place the scrolls on the table or box in the synagogue.

Bible ZONE®

Choose one or more activities to immerse your children in the Bible story.

Wonder Works

Have the children stand in your story area. Lead the children in the following movement activity.

Jesus grew from a baby,
(Rock baby in your arms.)
Just like me and you.
(Point to self; point to others.)
And when he grew into a boy,
(Crouch down, then stand up tall.)
I wonder what he could do?
(Put finger on the side of your head.)

I wonder if Jesus could . . .
   jump! Let's all jump.
I wonder if Jesus could . . .
   run! Let's all run in place.
I wonder if Jesus could . . .
   hop! Let's all hop on one foot.
I wonder if Jesus could . . .
   sit! Let's all sit down.

Say: Jesus grew from a baby to a boy to a man. Today our Bible story is about when Jesus was a man. Jesus went to the synagogue in his hometown. While he was there, he read from the Scriptures. He told the people that God wanted him to tell others the good news about God's love.

Supplies:
none

Zillies®:
none

Sign 'n Say

Teach the children the Bible verse, "Jesus grew both in body and in wisdom" (Luke 2:52, *Good News Bible*), in American Sign Language.

Jesus—Touch the middle finger of the right hand to the palm of the left hand. Reverse.

Grew—Let the thumb and fingers of the left hand form an open circle, with the palm facing right. Push the right open hand up through the left hand.

Body—Touch your chest with both open palms. Repeat the motion slightly lower on the body.

Wisdom—Bend the index finger of the right hand. Move the bent finger up and down in front of the forehead.

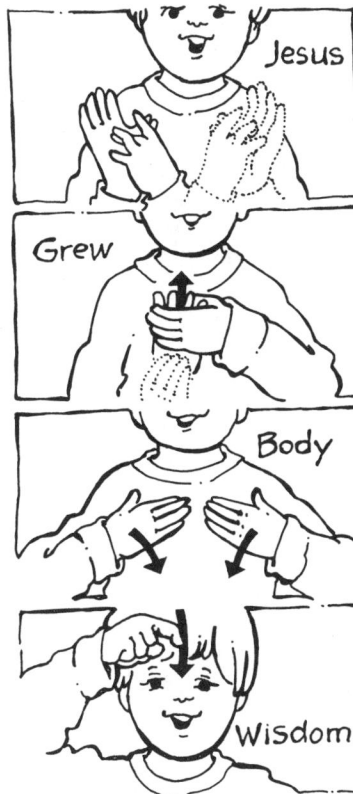

Jesus

Grew

Body

Wisdom

© 1998 Abingdon Press

Supplies:
none

Zillies®:

Step, Step, Step

by Daphna Flegal

Ⓟ *hotocopy and cut apart one set of the story pictures **(Reproducible 6A)**. Place the pictures in order.*

Have the children stand in a circle in the synagogue area. Show the children the pictures as indicated in the story. Have the children walk in place each time you say the "Step, step, step" verse.

(Show Picture 1, Jesus walking down the road.)
Jesus went to Nazareth, his hometown.

Step, step, step.
Step, step, step.
Jesus walked into town.

(Show Picture 2, the synagogue.)
He went to the synagogue. The synagogue was an important place to worship and to learn about God.

Step, step, step.
Step, step, step.
Jesus walked into the synagogue.

Jesus saw many people he knew in the synagogue. The people knew that he was Mary's son. The people knew that he had helped Joseph in the carpenter's shop.

(Show Picture 3, Jesus reading from the scroll.)
While Jesus was at the synagogue, he read from the Scriptures. The Scriptures were written on a scroll.

Step, step, step.
Step, step, step.
Jesus walked in front of the people to read the scroll.

"I have good news," said Jesus. "I have good news for the poor. I have good news for the sick. I have good news for the sad. God wants me to tell you the good news about God's love."

(Show Picture 4, Jesus walking out of town.)
The people in his hometown did not want to listen to Jesus. They became angry.

Step, step, step.
Step, step, step.
Jesus walked out of town.

Jesus left his hometown and went to tell others the good news about God's love.

Step, step, step.
Step, step, step.
Jesus walked to another town.

Many people listened to Jesus tell the good news about God's love.

Bible Verse Buzz

Choose a child to hold the Bible open to Luke 2:52.

Say: Jesus grew from a baby to a boy to a man. Today our Bible story is about when Jesus was a man. Jesus went to the synagogue in his hometown.

Say the Bible verse, "Jesus grew both in body and in wisdom" (Luke 2:52, *Good News Bible*), for the children. Have the children say the Bible verse after you.

Turn your back to the children or hide your hands underneath a table or behind the **BibleZone® FUNspirational® Kit** lid as you place the **BZ Bee puppet** (see page 174) on your hand. Turn around or bring the puppet out where the children can see it.

Pretend to make the puppet talk. Change your voice for the puppet:

Bzzz. Bzzz. Bzzz. Hi, everybody! I'm BZ Bee. *Bzzz. Bzzz. Bzzz.* I like to taste fingers. Do you have fingers? Yum, yum, yum. Let me taste.

Go to each child. Encourage, but do not force, each child to hold up his or her fingers. Have BZ pretend to taste each child's fingers. Have BZ say things like:

Mmmm. Mmmm. You taste like honey.
Bzzz. Bzzz. You taste like strawberries.
Yumm. Yumm. You taste like blueberries.

After BZ has tasted each child's fingers, say:

Bzzz. Bzzz. Bzzz. I like to taste your fingers. They're yummy. *(Rub BZ's stomach).*

Bzzz. Bzzz. Bzzz. I like something else even more than fingers.

I like the Bible. *Bzzz. Bzzz. Bzzz.* You heard a Bible story today. Who was the man in the story? *(Jesus)* Where did Jesus go in today's story? *(to the synagogue)* What did Jesus tell the people in the synagogue? *(good news about God's love)*

Bzzz. Bzzz. Bzzz. Jesus told the people the good news about God's love.

> ## We can tell others the good news about God's love.

Bzzz. Bzzz. Bzzz. Let's all say the Bible verse together.

"Jesus grew both in body and in wisdom" (Luke 2:52, *Good News Bible*).

Have the children repeat the Bible verse with BZ Bee.

Have BZ Bee say goodbye to the children. Put the puppet away.

Bible Zone®

Choose one or more activities to immerse your children in the Bible story.

Supplies:
cassette player

Zillies®:
Cassette

Sing!

Say: Today our Bible story is about when Jesus was a man. Jesus went to the synagogue. While he was there, he read from the Scriptures. The Scriptures were written on a scroll. Jesus told the people that God wanted him to tell them the good news about God's love. Let's sing a song about God's love.

Sing with the children the song "This Is My Commandment" from the **Cassette**.

This Is My Commandment

This is My commandment,
that you love one another,
that your joy may be full.

This is My commandment,
that you love one another,
that your joy may be full.

That your joy may be full,
that your joy may be full.

This is My commandment,
that you love one another,
that your joy may be full.

That your joy may be full,
that your joy may be full.

This is My commandment,
that you love one another,
that your joy may be full.

That your joy may be full.

Life Zone

Choose one or more activities to bring the Bible to life.

Unroll the Scroll

Have the children sit down in the synagogue area. Give each child her or his scroll **(Reproducible 6A)**.

Say: **Today our Bible story is about when Jesus was a man. Jesus went to the synagogue. While he was there, he read from the Scriptures. The Scriptures were written on a scroll. Jesus told the people that God wanted him to tell them the good news about God's love.**

> ## We can tell others the good news about God's love.

Choose a child to begin the activity.

Say: **(Child's name), tell the good news.**

Have the child stand up, unroll the scroll, and say, "God loves you!" Then have the child sit back down. If you have a large group of children, have two or three children do this activity at a time.

Supplies:
scrolls
(Reproducible 6A)

Zillies®:
none

Good News Games

Photocopy the good news giraffes **(Reproducible 6B)**. Cut the giraffes apart along the solid line. Each child will need one giraffe. Roll each giraffe into a tube and tape the ends together.

Have the children move to one side of the room. Place a long line of masking tape on the floor on the other side of the room. (If you have younger children, make the line closer to where the children are starting.) Give each child a giraffe.

Say: **These are good news giraffes. They want to tell others the good news about God's love, but they need our help. Get down on your hands and knees and blow your giraffe. The giraffe will roll along the floor. Keep blowing until your giraffe rolls across the finish line. When you get to the finish line, shout, "God loves you!"**

Show the children how to blow on the giraffe to make it roll. Continue the game as long as the children show interest.

Supplies:
Reproducible 6B,
scissors, clear tape,
masking tape

Zillies®:

Life Zone

Choose one or more activities to bring the Bible to life.

Supplies:
none

Zillies®:
none

Bible Verse Sing-along

Have the children sit in a circle on the floor.

Say: Jesus grew just like we grow. He grew from a baby to a boy to a man. As Jesus grew, he learned about God.

Sing the Bible verse with the children. The tune is "Hot Cross Buns."

Jesus grew.
Jesus grew.
Both in body and in wisdom,
Jesus grew.

Supplies:
none

Zillies®:
inflatable feather pillow

Pillow Prayers

Have the children sit in a circle on the floor.

Say: Jesus grew from a baby to a boy to a man. When Jesus was a man, he was baptized with water from a river. As Jesus was baptized, a dove flew down from the sky, and a voice spoke. The voice told Jesus that God loved him and that he was God's Son. After he was baptized, he went to the synagogue in his hometown. Jesus read from a scroll and told the people the good news about God's love.

Show the children the **inflatable feather pillow.**

Say: The feathers in our pillow can remind us about the dove. We can remember that the Bible tells us Jesus is God's Son.

Pass the pillow around the circle. As each child holds the pillow, have the child **say, "Jesus is God's Son."**

Pray: Thank you, God, for loving (name each child). Amen.

Photocopy the **HomeZone**® newsletter to send home to parents.

78

BIBLEZONE®

Bible Verse
Jesus grew both in body and in wisdom.
Luke 2:52, *Good News Bible*

Bible Story
Luke 4:16–30; Matthew 13:54–58; Mark 6:1–6

At the Synagogue

Today your child heard the story of when Jesus went to the synagogue in his hometown of Nazareth. The synagogue was an important place to worship and to learn about God. It was the school for boys, the meeting hall, and the courtroom, as well as the place for sabbath worship. Services, which included prayer, praise, reading of the scrolls, and instruction, were held every sabbath day.

When Jesus visited the synagogue in Nazareth, he was invited to read from the scrolls, rolls of heavy parchment that contained the Scriptures. After he read the Scriptures, Jesus announced that he was the fulfillment of the Scriptures. God wanted him to bring good news to the poor, to the needy, and to the sad.

What is the good news for preschool children? The good news is that God loves each one of them.

Synagogue Snack

Enjoy making this Bible-times snack with your child. Share the snack with a neighbor or friend. Tell the neighbor or friend the good news about God's love.

2 cups pitted dates
2 cups walnuts
butter or margarine
powdered sugar

Chop the dates and walnuts very fine. Mix the dates and walnuts together, rubbing with the back of a spoon until smooth.

Place a piece of wax paper on the counter or table. Wipe butter on your child's hands. Let your child roll the mixture into balls on the wax paper. Then let your child sprinkle the balls with powdered sugar.

ZONE IN
We can tell others the good news about God's love.

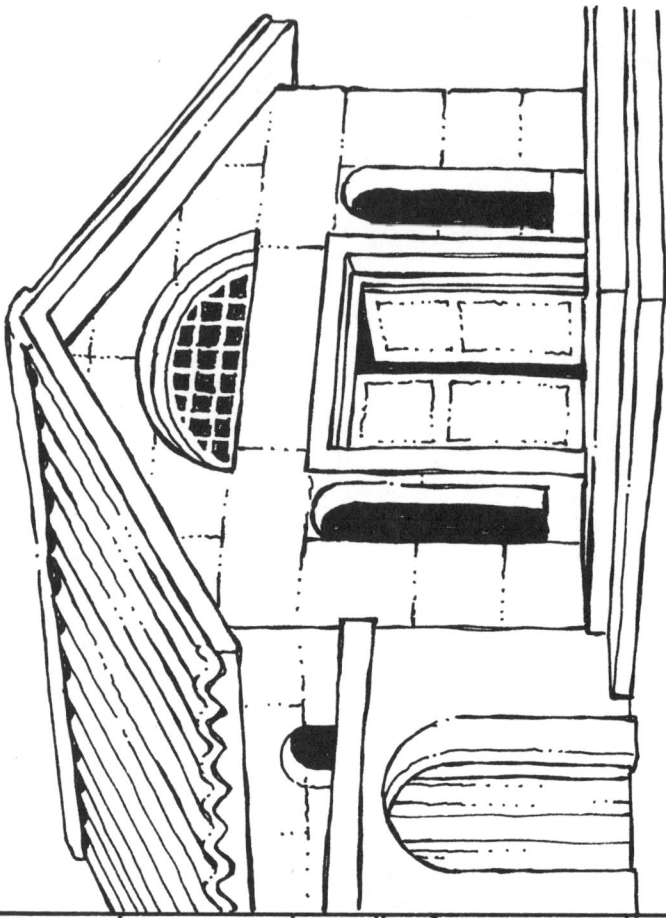

2

4

1

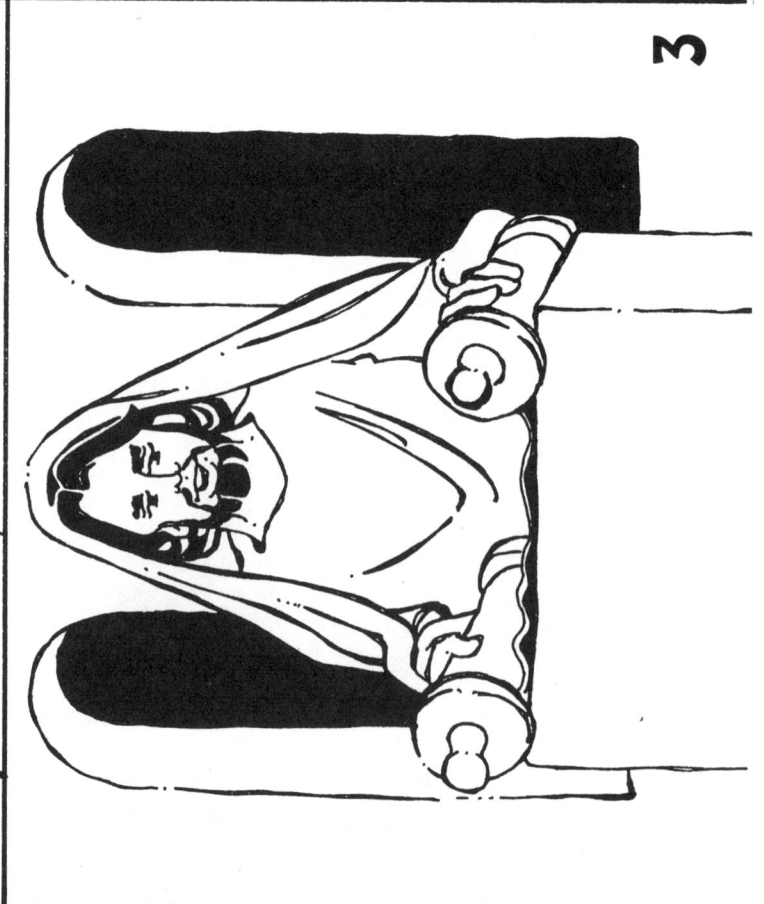

3

Reproducible 6A

BIBLEZONE®

Reproducible 6B

81

By the Sea

Enter the ZONE

Bible Verse
And Jesus said to them, "Follow me."
Mark 1:17

Bible Story
Luke 5:1–11; Matthew 4:18–22; Mark 1:16–20

After Jesus' rejection at Nazareth he went to the city of Capernaum. From the shores of the Sea of Galilee, he recruited his first disciples.

Disciples of great teachers were not uncommon. Often after years of study, a boy would associate himself with a teacher whose life was dedicated to teaching and meditation. He would become a "disciple" of the teacher. It was also known for a teacher to call talented students to be disciples.

However, it was uncommon for a teacher to call those who didn't seem to be particularly interested in a disciple's lifestyle or who did not seem to have great affinity for lifelong study.

Jesus did not call talented students or the elite of society. He called working men.

We often talk about the "poor" fishermen. But these were busy men who made a living fishing. They were working-class people. They were not rich, but they had full lives. The extraordinary thing is that these ordinary men left jobs, families, and possessions to learn at the feet of Jesus and to pass on that learning.

Earning a living and building an ordinary life were no longer their focus. After their call these men traveled with Jesus, depending upon the hospitality of others.

The four fishermen that Jesus called from the Sea of Galilee became part of his core group, those to whom carrying on the word of the kingdom of God was entrusted.

Sometimes we feel that it takes extraordinary people to do great things. Yet Jesus called four ordinary fishermen to be his disciples. God used these ordinary people to do great things. You are called to be a disciple. God can work through you as a teacher to achieve great things and to make God's love known to the children.

We can tell others the good news about God's love.

Scope the ZONE ®

ZONE	TIME	SUPPLIES	⊚ ZILLIES®
Zoom Into the Zone			
Gone Fishing	15 minutes	Reproducible 7A, lunch-size paper bags, crayons or markers, netting, vegetable or fruit mesh bags, yarn or string, glue, scissors	none
Fish Frenzy	5 minutes	fish (Reproducible 7A)	none
BibleZone®			
Hop 'n Stop	5 minutes	none	none
Splash, Splash, Splash	10 minutes	none	none
Bible Verse Buzz	5 minutes	Bible, BZ Bee	none
Sing!	5 minutes	cassette player	Cassette
LifeZone			
Seascapes	15 minutes	Reproducible 7B, newspaper, paint smocks, crayons, blue tempera paint, shallow trays; spoon, drinking straws; yarn, scissors; water, paintbrush	none
Swim, Little Fish	10 minutes	none	none
A Fishing Song	5 minutes	none	none
Sign 'n Pray	5 minutes	none	none

⊚ Zillies® are found in the **BibleZone® FUNspirational® Kit.**

Zoom Into the ZONE®

Choose one or more activities to catch your children's interest.

Supplies:
Reproducible 7A,
lunch-size paper
bags, crayons or
markers, netting,
vegetable or fruit
mesh bags, yarn or
string, glue, scissors

Zillies®:
none

Gone Fishing

(P) hotocopy and cut apart several copies of the fish **(Reproducible 7A)**. Hide the fish around the room before the children arrive.

Give each child a small paper bag. Let the children decorate the bags with crayons or markers.

Cut netting, vegetable or fruit mesh bags, and yarn or string into small pieces. Let the children glue the pieces onto the outside of their paper bags.

Say: **Today our Bible story is about when Jesus saw fishermen using their nets to catch fish. Jesus asked the fishermen to stop fishing and to follow him. Jesus wanted the fishermen to help him tell others the good news about God's love.**

ZONE IN®

We can tell others the good news about God's love.

Have the children hold their fish-net bags.

Say: **Let's pretend that we are fishermen and that our bags are our fishing nets. Look all around the room. When you find a paper fish, pick it up and put it in your net.**

Encourage the children to look for the fish you have hidden around the room. Sing the song printed below to the tune of "This Is the Way" as the children find the fish.

> This is the way we catch our fish,
> Catch our fish, catch our fish.
> This is the way we catch our fish
> In our fishing nets.

Supplies:
fish (Reproducible
7A)

Zillies®:
none

Fish Frenzy

(H) ave the children bring their fish **(Reproducible 7A)** back to the table or to the rug. Encourage the children to pour all their fish out into a pile. Then have the children work together to match the fish pictures.

Bible ZONE

Choose one or more activities to immerse your children in the Bible story.

Hop 'n Stop

Have the children line up behind you. Lead the children around the room as you say the verse printed below. Encourage the children to do the motions as you do. Have the children repeat the Bible verse after you each time. Lead the children to your story area.

Supplies:
none

Zillies®:
none

Come, follow me
And hop, hop, hop,
(Hop around the room.)
Hop, hop, hop,
Hop, hop, hop.
Come, follow me
And hop, hop, hop.
Hop until I stop.
(Stop.)

Come, *(name each child).*
Jesus said, "Come, follow me."
(Motion "come here" with your arm.)

Come, follow me
And march, march, march,
(March around the room.)
March, march, march,
March, march, march.
Come, follow me
And march, march, march.
March until I stop.
(Stop.)

Come, *(name each child).*
Jesus said, "Come, follow me."
(Motion "come here" with your arm.)

Come, follow me
And tip-tip toe,
(Tiptoe around the room.)
Tip-tiptoe,
Tip-tiptoe.
Come, follow me
And tip-tiptoe.
Tiptoe until I stop.
(Stop; have the children sit down in your story area.)

Splash, Splash, Splash

by Daphna Flegal

*H*ave the children sit down in your story area. Let the children rock back and forth as if they were riding in a boat each time you say, "Splash, splash, splash."

Splash, splash, splash. The waves splashed to the shore. Jesus was standing beside the sea. Many, many people were crowding around him. Many, many people wanted to hear Jesus tell the good news about God's love.

Splash, splash, splash. The waves splashed against two boats on the sand by the sea. Fisherman Peter and his friends were beside the boats, washing their nets.

Splash, splash, splash. The waves splashed as Jesus stepped into Peter's boat. He asked Peter to take the boat out onto the lake. Jesus taught the many, many people from the boat. He told the people the good news about God's love.

Splash, splash, splash. The waves splashed as they rocked the boat back and forth in the water.

"Take the boat farther out," Jesus said to Peter. "Put your nets into the deep water, and you will catch some fish."

"We have already fished all night," said Peter. "We did not catch any fish at all. But we can put out our nets and try again."

Splash, splash, splash. The waves splashed as Fisherman Peter put his nets in the water.

Splash, splash, splash. The waves splashed as fish swam into the net. There were lots and lots of fish. Fisherman Peter was surprised!

Splash, splash, splash. The waves splashed over the nets filled with fish as Peter called to his friends to come and help him. The friends rowed their boats to help Peter. Soon their nets were filled with even more fish. There were so many fish that the boats began to sink!

Splash, splash, splash. The waves splashed against the boats as the fishermen rowed back to shore.

"Come, follow me," said Jesus to the fishermen. "I want you to fish for people. I want you to help me tell others the good news about God's love."

Splash, splash, splash. The waves splashed against the sand as Fisherman Peter and his friends left their boats to follow Jesus.

Bible Verse Buzz

Choose a child to hold the Bible open to Mark 1:17.

Say: Today our Bible story is about when Jesus saw four fishermen using their nets to catch fish. Jesus asked the fishermen to stop fishing and to follow him.

Say the Bible verse, "And Jesus said to them, 'Follow me'" (Mark 1:17), for the children. Have the children say the Bible verse after you.

Turn your back to the children or hide your hands underneath a table or behind the **BibleZone® FUNspirational® Kit** lid as you place the **BZ Bee puppet** (see page 174) on your hand. Turn around or bring the puppet out where the children can see it.

Pretend to make the puppet talk. Change your voice for the puppet:

Bzzz. Bzzz. Bzzz. Hi, everybody! I'm BZ Bee. *Bzzz. Bzzz. Bzzz.* I like to taste fingers. Do you have fingers? Yum, yum, yum. Let me taste.

Go to each child. Encourage, but do not force, each child to hold up his or her fingers. Have BZ pretend to taste each child's fingers. Have BZ say things like:

Mmmm. Mmmm. You taste like honey. *Bzzz. Bzzz.* You taste like strawberries. *Yumm. Yumm.* You taste like blueberries.

After BZ has tasted each child's fingers, say:

Bzzz. Bzzz. Bzzz. I like to taste your fingers. They're yummy. *(Rub BZ's stomach).*

Bzzz. Bzzz. Bzzz. I like something else even more than fingers.

I like the Bible. *Bzzz. Bzzz. Bzzz.* You heard a Bible story today. Who was the man in the story? *(Jesus)* What did Jesus do in today's story? *(asked the fishermen to help him)* What did Jesus want the fishermen to do? *(fish for people; tell the good news about God's love)*

Bzzz. Bzzz. Bzzz. Jesus wanted the fishermen to help him tell others the good news about God's love.

We can tell others the good news about God's love.

Bzzz. Bzzz. Bzzz. Let's all say the Bible verse together.

"And Jesus said to them, 'Follow me'" (Mark 1:17).

Have the children repeat the Bible verse with BZ Bee.

Have BZ Bee say goodbye to the children. Put the puppet away.

Choose one or more activities to immerse your children in the Bible story.

Supplies:
cassette player

Zillies®:
Cassette

Sing!

(P) lay the song "Twelve Disciples" from the **Cassette.** Encourage the children to count along with the song.

Twelve Disciples

1 - 2 - 3 - 4 - 5 Disciples,
6 - 7 - 8 - 9 - 10 Disciples,
two more men make 12 Disciples,
12 Disciples of Jesus.

Jesus looked for friends to help Him,
Jesus looked for friends to help Him,
Jesus looked for friends to help Him,
12 Disciples of Jesus.

1 - 2 - 3 - 4 - 5 Disciples,
6 - 7 - 8 - 9 - 10 Disciples,
two more men make 12 Disciples,
12 Disciples of Jesus.

Peter, James, John and Andrew,
Four Disciples, then we come to
Philip, Thaddeus, Thomas, Matthew,
12 Disciples of Jesus.

James, Bartholomew, one named Simon,
loved the Lord, stayed close beside Him,
'cept for Judas who denied Him,
12 Disciples of Jesus.

1 - 2 - 3 - 4 - 5 Disciples,
6 - 7 - 8 - 9 - 10 Disciples,
two more men make 12 Disciples,
12 Disciples of Jesus.

Writer: Dennis Scott
© 1989 New Spring Publishing, Inc. (ASCAP) (a div. of Brentwood-Benson Music Publishing, Inc.)
All Rights Reserved. Used by Permission.

From the Brentwood-Benson Music Publishing, Inc. recording, *Mother Goose Gospel, Vol. 2.*

Seascapes

Photocopy the Bible verse picture **(Reproducible 7B)** for each child. Cover the table with newspapers and have the children wear paint smocks. Give each child a picture. Let the children color the pictures with crayons. Read the Bible verse for the children.

Say: Today our Bible story is about when Jesus saw fishermen using their nets to catch fish. Jesus asked the fishermen to stop fishing and to follow him. Jesus wanted the fishermen to help him tell others the good news about God's love.

Let the children add waves and water to their pictures in one of the following ways:

Blow painting. Pour blue tempera paint into shallow trays. Spoon a small amount of paint onto each child's picture. Show the children how to blow the paint through straws to make waves. Make sure the children know how to blow, not suck, through the straws.

Yarn painting. Pour blue tempera paint into shallow trays. Cut yarn into eight-inch lengths. Show the children how to dip the yarn into the paint and then pull the yarn over their pictures to make wavy lines.

Paint wash. Thin blue tempera paint with water. Show the children how to use paintbrushes to paint the thinned tempera over their pictures to make the sea.

Lay the pictures flat to dry.

Supplies:
Reproducible 7B, newspaper, paint smocks, crayons, blue tempera paint, shallow trays; spoon, drinking straws; yarn, scissors; water, paintbrushes

Zillies®:
none

Swim, Little Fish

Have the children move to one side of the room. Tell the children to pretend that they are fish and that you are the fisherman. Stand in the middle of the room and say the poem printed below. When you say, "Swim to me," have the children try to swim past you to get to the other side of the room. Tag the children as they move. Have any children you tag stay with you and become fishermen. Continue the game until all the fish are caught.

I'm a fisherman, as you can see. Swim, little fish, swim to me.

Supplies:
none

Zillies®:

Life Zone®

Choose one or more activities to bring the Bible to life.

Supplies:
none

Zillies®:
none

A Fishing Song

Have the children sit down in a circle on the floor.

Say: **Today our Bible story is about when Jesus saw fishermen using their nets to catch fish. Jesus asked the fishermen to stop fishing and to follow him. Jesus wanted the fishermen to help him tell others the good news about God's love. Let's sing a song about the four fishermen. Their names are Peter, Andrew, James, and John.**

Teach the children the song "Jesus Called Four Fishermen" to the tune of "Twinkle, Twinkle, Little Star."

> Jesus called four fishermen:
> Peter, Andrew, James, and John.
> "Follow me; for if you do,
> You will fish for people too."
> Jesus called four fishermen:
> Peter, Andrew, James, and John.

Words by Sharilyn S. Adair
© 1997 by Cokesbury.

Supplies:
none

Zillies®:
none

Follow—Make a fist with both hands, thumbs out. Hold the right fist behind the left fist. Move both fists forward. Me—Point index finger of the right hand toward your chest.

Sign 'n Pray

Have the children sit in a circle on the floor. Teach the children the Bible verse in American Sign Language. Go around the circle and name each child.

Say: *(Child's name)*, **Jesus said, "Come, follow me."**

Have the child sign the verse with you.

© 1998 Abingdon Press

Pray: **Thank you, God, for the good news that you love** *(name each child and teacher)*. **Amen.**

Photocopy the **HomeZone**® newsletter to send home to parents.

Beside the Sea

Today your child heard the Bible story of when Jesus called the fishermen. He told them that he wanted them to leave their boats and to fish for people.

It was not uncommon in Bible times for teachers to call students to learn from them. It was uncommon, however, to call students from the working class like the fishermen.

Sometimes we feel that it takes extraordinary people to do great things. Yet Jesus called four ordinary fishermen to be his disciples. God used these ordinary people to do great things. You are called to be a disciple. God can work through you as a parent or grandparent to achieve great things and to make God's love known to your child.

Bible Verse
And Jesus said to them, "Follow me." Mark 1:17

Bible Story
Luke 5:1–11; Matthew 4:18–22; Mark 1:16–20

A Fishing Song

Help your child learn the names of the four fishermen who followed Jesus. Sing the song "Jesus Called Four Fishermen" to the tune of "Twinkle, Twinkle, Little Star."

Jesus called four fishermen:
Peter, Andrew, James, and John.
"Follow me; for if you do,
You will fish for people too."
Jesus called four fishermen:
Peter, Andrew, James, and John.

Words by Sharilyn S. Adair
© 1997 by Cokesbury.

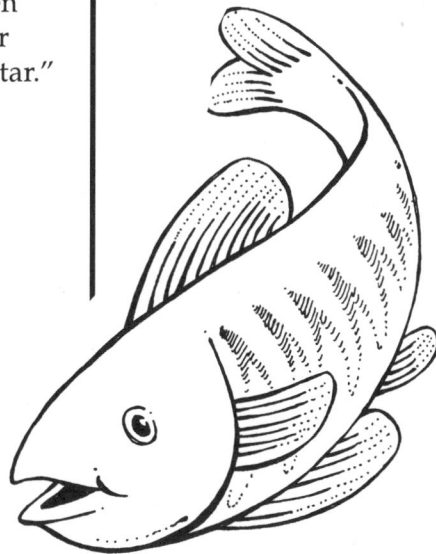

Zone In

We can tell others the good news about God's love.

Permission granted to photocopy for local church use. © 1999 Abingdon Press.

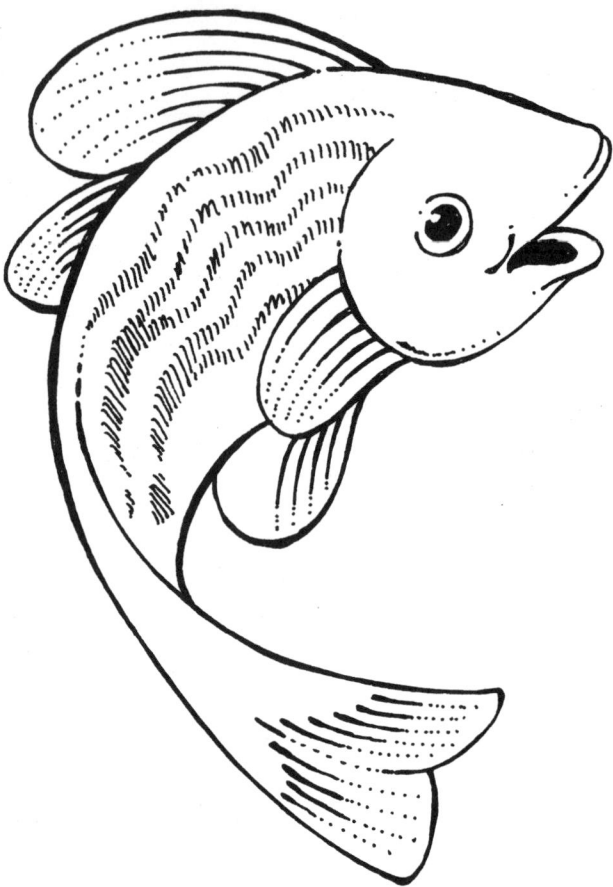

Reproducible 7A

BibleZone®

And Jesus said to them, "Follow me."
Mark 1:17

Reproducible 7B

On the Hillside

Enter the ZONE

Bible Verse
And Jesus said to them, "Follow me."
Mark 1:17

Bible Story
Matthew 5:1–7:28

Jesus went up on the mountain to give the sermon that contains his core teachings, the Sermon on the Mount. This sermon may have been given at one time, or it may be a compilation of his most often taught principles.

Matthew 5:1-12 and Luke 6:20-26 are a recounting of the Beatitudes, a main teaching of the Sermon on the Mount. The Beatitudes are a listing of the "attitudes" that lead to being blessed in the sight of God.

Many pages of commentary can be found on each of these Beatitudes. The overall meaning of the Beatitudes is our attitude toward life and God. The Beatitudes turn worldly thinking upside down. They change our values into God's values.

The second group of teachings deals with the nature of discipleship—love your enemy; do not worry, for God cares for you; the Lord's Prayer; and do to others as you would have them do to you. Jesus' words shocked the people of his day. But Jesus wanted to be very clear: All who wanted to be true disciples must live by these teach-

ings. If we are to follow Jesus, we must follow his teachings in our relationship with God and others.

Young children are concrete thinkers. They will have trouble understanding the abstract concepts of Jesus' teachings. The goal in this lesson is to show the children that Jesus was a special teacher who taught the good news about God's love. Many people listened to Jesus and followed him. We can listen to Jesus' teachings and follow him.

We can listen to Jesus' teachings and follow him.

Scope the ZONE

ZONE	TIME	SUPPLIES	⦿ ZILLIES®
Zoom Into the Zone			
Picture Pairs	5 minutes	Reproducible 8A, scissors	none
Hillside Happening	15 minutes	Reproducible 8B, crayons or markers, cotton balls, glue, colored tissue paper, scissors, shallow containers, cotton swabs	none
BibleZone®			
Hop 'n Stop	5 minutes	none	none
Five Teachings	10 minutes	none	none
Bible Verse Buzz	5 minutes	Bible, BZ Bee	none
Sing!	5 minutes	cassette player	Cassette
LifeZone			
Up the Hillside	10 minutes	Reproducible 8B, tape, chair	none
Who's on the Hillside?	10 minutes	chair	none
Bible Verse Sing-along	5 minutes	none	none
Sign 'n Pray	5 minutes	none	none

⦿ Zillies® are found in the **BibleZone® FUNspirational® Kit.**

Zoom Into the ZONE

Choose one or more activities to catch your children's interest.

Supplies:
Reproducible 8A,
scissors

Zillies®:
none

Picture Pairs

P hotocopy and cut apart at least two copies of the pictures (**Reproducible 8A**). Mix up the pictures and place them on the table or rug. Let the children match the pictures.

Say: Today our Bible story is about a time when Jesus taught on a hillside. Let's pretend we are on the hillside in Bible times. What do you think we would see?

Let the children think of their own answers. Then show the children the pictures of Jesus teaching (sitting on a rock), the crowd of people, the disciples or Jesus' helpers, birds, the rabbit, and wildflowers.

Say: Many people came to the hillside to listen to Jesus' teachings and to follow him.

> **We can listen to Jesus' teachings and follow him.**

Supplies:
Reproducible 8B,
crayons or markers,
cotton balls, glue,
colored tissue paper,
scissors, shallow
containers, cotton
swabs

Zillies®:
none

Hillside Happening

P hotocopy the hillside picture (**Reproducible 8B**) for each child. Let the children color the pictures with crayons or markers.

Let the children add clouds to the sky by gluing on cotton balls. Let the children add flowers with colored tissue paper. Cut tissue paper into two-inch squares. Pour glue into shallow containers and provide cotton swabs. Show the children how to crumple the squares into balls. Then show the children how to place a dot of glue on their papers with the cotton swabs and to press the crumpled tissue paper on the glue. Encourage the children to make lots of different colored flowers on their hillside pictures.

Say: Today our Bible story is about a time when Jesus taught on a hillside. Many people came to the hillside to listen to Jesus' teachings and to follow him.

Choose one or more activities to immerse your children in the Bible story.

Hop 'n Stop

Supplies:
none

Zillies®:
none

Have the children line up behind you. Lead the children around the room as you say the verse printed below. Encourage the children to do the motions as you do. Have the children repeat the Bible verse after you each time. Lead the children to your story area.

Come, follow me
And hop, hop, hop,
(Hop around the room.)
Hop, hop, hop,
Hop, hop, hop.
Come, follow me
And hop, hop, hop.
Hop until I stop.
(Stop.)

Come, *(name each child).*
Jesus said, "Come, follow me."
(Motion "come here" with your arm.)

Come, follow me
And march, march, march,
(March around the room.)
March, march, march,
March, march, march.
Come, follow me
And march, march, march.
March until I stop.
(Stop.)

Come, *(name each child).*
Jesus said, "Come, follow me."
(Motion "come here" with your arm.)

Come, follow me
And tip-tiptoe,
(Tiptoe around the room.)
Tip-tiptoe,
Tip-tiptoe.
Come, follow me
And tip-tiptoe.
Tiptoe until I stop.
(Stop; have the children sit down in your story area.)

Five Teachings

by Daphna Flegal

Have the children sit down in your story area. Practice the motions for the "Give me five" refrain with the children. Then tell the story and have the children do the suggested motions with you.

One day Jesus went up on the hillside. His helpers followed him up the hillside. They wanted to hear Jesus' teachings. They wanted to follow Jesus.

Give me five.
(Hold up one hand, fingers spread apart.)
Give me five.
(Hold up other hand, fingers spread apart.)
Give me five of Jesus' teachings.
(Shake both hands in the air.)

1. Jesus taught about how to be happy.
(Hold up one finger.)

2. Jesus taught about how to love others.
(Hold up two fingers.)

3. Jesus taught about how to pray.
(Hold up three fingers.)

4. Jesus taught about how God cares for us.
(Hold up four fingers.)

5. Jesus taught about how to treat others.
(Hold up five fingers.)

Give me five.
(Hold up one hand, fingers spread apart.)
Give me five.
(Hold up other hand, fingers spread apart.)
Give me five of Jesus' teachings.
(Shake both hands in the air.)

Many people followed Jesus and his helpers up the hillside. They wanted to hear Jesus' teachings. They wanted to follow Jesus.

Give me five.
(Hold up one hand, fingers spread apart.)
Give me five.
(Hold up other hand, fingers spread apart.)
Give me five of Jesus' teachings.
(Shake both hands in the air.)

1. Jesus taught about how to be happy.
(Hold up one finger.)

2. Jesus taught about how to love others.
(Hold up two fingers.)

3. Jesus taught about how to pray.
(Hold up three fingers.)

4. Jesus taught about how God cares for us.
(Hold up four fingers.)

5. Jesus taught about how to treat others.
(Hold up five fingers.)

Give me five.
(Hold up one hand, fingers spread apart.)
Give me five.
(Hold up other hand, fingers spread apart.)
Give me five of Jesus' teachings.
(Shake both hands in the air.)

Bible Verse Buzz

Choose a child to hold the Bible open to Mark 1:17.

Say: Today our Bible story is about when Jesus taught on the hillside. Many people came to the hillside to hear Jesus' teachings. Many people wanted to follow Jesus.

Say the Bible verse, "And Jesus said to them, 'Follow me'" (Mark 1:17), for the children. Have the children say the Bible verse after you.

Turn your back to the children or hide your hands underneath a table or behind the **BibleZone® FUNspirational® Kit** lid as you place the **BZ Bee puppet** (see page 174) on your hand. Turn around or bring the puppet out where the children can see it.

Pretend to make the puppet talk. Change your voice for the puppet:

Bzzz. Bzzz. Bzzz. Hi, everybody! I'm BZ Bee. *Bzzz. Bzzz. Bzzz.* I like to taste fingers. Do you have fingers? Yum, yum, yum. Let me taste.

Go to each child. Encourage, but do not force, each child to hold up his or her fingers. Have BZ pretend to taste each child's fingers. Have BZ say things like:

Mmmm. Mmmm. You taste like honey. *Bzzz. Bzzz.* You taste like strawberries. *Yumm. Yumm.* You taste like blueberries.

After BZ has tasted each child's fingers, say:

Bzzz. Bzzz. Bzzz. I like to taste your fingers. They're yummy. (*Rub BZ's stomach*).

Bzzz. Bzzz. Bzzz. I like something else even more than fingers.

I like the Bible. *Bzzz. Bzzz. Bzzz.* You heard a Bible story today. Who was the man in the story? (*Jesus*) Where did Jesus teach in today's story? (*on the hillside*)

Bzzz. Bzzz. Bzzz. Jesus taught about God. Many people listened to Jesus' teachings and wanted to follow Jesus.

> **Zone IN**
> **We can listen to Jesus' teachings and follow him.**

Bzzz. Bzzz. Bzzz. Let's all say the Bible verse together.

"And Jesus said to them, 'Follow me'" (Mark 1:17).

Have the children repeat the Bible verse with BZ Bee.

Have BZ Bee say goodbye to the children.

Bible ZONE

Choose one or more activities to immerse your children in the Bible story.

Supplies:
cassette player

Zillies®:
Cassette

Sing!

Say: Today our Bible story is about when Jesus taught on the hill-side. Many people came to the hillside to hear Jesus' teachings. Some of Jesus' teachings were about love. Let's sing a song about love.

Sing with the children the song "This Is My Commandment" from the **Cassette.**

This Is My Commandment

This is My commandment,
that you love one another,
that your joy may be full.

This is My commandment,
that you love one another,
that your joy may be full.

That your joy may be full,
that your joy may be full.

This is My commandment,
that you love one another,
that your joy may be full.

That your joy may be full,
that your joy may be full.

This is My commandment,
that you love one another,
that your joy may be full.

That your joy may be full.

Up the Hillside

Supplies:
Reproducible 8B,
tape, chair

Zillies®:
none

(P) hotocopy one copy of the hillside picture **(Reproducible 8B)**. Tape the picture on a chair. Place the chair on one side of the room. Stand by the chair.

Say: **Today our Bible story is about when Jesus taught on the hillside. Many people came to the hillside to hear Jesus' teachings. Many people wanted to follow Jesus.**

ZONE IN

We can listen to Jesus' teachings and follow him.

Have the children move to the side of the room across from the chair.

Say: **Let's pretend that we are Bible-times people going up the hillside to see Jesus. I will turn my back to you. When I turn my back, crawl to the hillside picture on the chair. When I turn back around, you must stop crawling.**

Turn around and have the children crawl toward the picture. After a few seconds turn back around. Have the children stop crawling. Continue the game, changing how the children move (jump, tiptoe, walk backwards, take baby steps, take giant steps, hop on one foot, and so forth).

When the children reach the chair, have all the children sit down around the chair. Sit in the chair and repeat the refrain and motions from today's Bible story with the children (see page 98).

Who's on the Hillside?

Supplies:
chair

Zillies®:
none

(C) ontinue to sit in the chair with the children seated on the floor around you.

Say: **I see someone on the hillside who can listen to Jesus' teachings and follow him.**

Describe a child. Keep describing the child until the children guess who you are describing. Continue the game until you have described every child.

Life Zone®

Supplies:
none

Zillies®:
none

Bible Verse Sing-a-long

Have the children sit down in a circle on the floor.

Say: Today our Bible story is about when Jesus taught on the hillside. Many people came to the hillside to hear Jesus' teachings. Many people wanted to follow Jesus.

Teach the children the song "Follow Me" to the tune of "Hot Cross Buns."

"Follow me."
"Follow me."
Jesus said to his disciples,
"Follow me."

© 1999 by Abingdon Press.

Supplies:
none

Zillies®:
none

Follow—Make a fist with both hands, thumbs out. Hold the right fist behind the left fist. Move both fists forward. Me—Point index finger of the right hand toward your chest.

Sign 'n Pray

Have the children sit in a circle on the floor. Teach the children the Bible verse in American Sign Language. Go around the circle and name each child.

Say: *(Child's name),* **Jesus said, "Come, follow me."**

Have the child sign the verse with you.

Pray: Thank you, God, for the good news that you love *(name each child and teacher).* **Amen.**

© 1998 Abingdon Press

Photocopy the **HomeZone**® newsletter to send home to parents.

BibleZone®

Home Zone® For Parents

On the Hillside

Today your child heard the story of when Jesus went up on the mountain to give the sermon that contains his core teachings, the Sermon on the Mount.

These teachings include the Beatitudes; love your enemy; do not worry, for God cares for you; the Lord's Prayer; and do to others as you would have them do to you.

Many people listened to Jesus and followed him. We can listen to Jesus' teachings and follow him.

Bible Verse
And Jesus said to them, "Follow me."   Mark 1:17

Bible Story
Matthew 5:1–7:28

Five Teachings

Help your child remember five of Jesus' teachings from the Sermon on the Mount. Say the verse printed below and do the motions with your child.

Give me five.
(Hold up one hand, fingers spread apart.)
Give me five.
(Hold up other hand, fingers spread apart.)
Give me five of Jesus' teachings.
(Shake both hands in the air.)

1. Jesus taught about how to be happy.
(Hold up one finger.)

2. Jesus taught about how to love others.
(Hold up two fingers.)

3. Jesus taught about how to pray.
(Hold up three fingers.)

4. Jesus taught about how God cares for us. *(Hold up four fingers.)*

5. Jesus taught about how to treat others.
(Hold up five fingers.)

We can listen to Jesus' teachings and follow him.

Reproducible 8A

BiBLeZONe®

Reproducible 8B

105

Through the Roof

Enter the ZONE®

Bible Verse
And Jesus said to them, "Follow me."
Mark 1:17

Bible Story
Luke 5:17-26; Matthew 9:2-8; Mark 2:1-12

On the ancient near East it was often thought that disease was caused by sin, especially disease that could not be cured.

It was not unusual for people who had exhausted all normal channels to cure illness to travel long distances for a cure. They would seek out a holy man who was reputed to perform healing miracles. Jesus already had a reputation for performing miracles.

Often forgotten is that it took four concerned, loving friends to carry the sick man to this healer, and that they went to a lot of trouble to do so. They had to take him on a pallet. When they arrived, there was such a large crowd, they couldn't get through. They then had to carry him up on the roof and tear away enough of the roof to lower the man to Jesus.

It is a testament to their faith that they went to this much trouble. They wouldn't have done so if they had thought it was futile. It was the faith of these four friends that Jesus rewarded by healing the sick man, though the man also showed faith.

Jesus upset the establishment not because he healed the man, but because he forgave the man's sins. Only God could forgive sins. By healing the man in this manner, Jesus proved that he had divine authority.

Jesus' show of divine authority caused trouble. His healing symbolized the coming of the kingdom of God. This was something the religious establishment couldn't accept. The man, however, went home praising God. We can only assume that his friends did the same.

Young children will have varying experiences with sickness, injury, or disabilities involving themselves, family members, or others. We want children to be assured that illness is not a punishment. Sickness, injury, and disabilities are not evidence of a lack of God's love. God loves everyone, and Jesus loved and cared for all people.

We can follow Jesus.

Scope the ZONE ®

ZONE	TIME	SUPPLIES	⊙ ZILLIES®
Zoom Into the Zone			
Open House	10 minutes	Reproducible 9A, tape, scissors, crayons or markers	sandpaper
The Friendly Four	10 minutes	construction paper, crayons	smile face beanbag key chains
BibleZone®			
Hop 'n Stop	5 minutes	none	none
The Hole in the Roof	10 minutes	Bible-times house (Reproducible 9A)	sandpaper, smile face beanbag key chains
Bible Verse Buzz	5 minutes	Bible, BZ Bee	none
Sing!	5 minutes	cassette player	Cassette
LifeZone			
House Hop	10 minutes	Bible-times house (Reproducible 9A)	sandpaper, smile face beanbag key chains
Ankle Bracelets	10 minutes	Reproducible 9B, scissors, tape	none
Bible Verse Sing-along	5 minutes	none	none
Sign 'n Pray	5 minutes	none	none

⊙ Zillies® are found in the **BibleZone® FUNspirational® Kit.**

Zoom Into the Zone

Choose one or more activities to catch your children's interest.

Supplies:
Reproducible 9A, tape, scissors, crayons or markers

Zillies®:
sandpaper

Open House

Photocopy four copies of the Bible-times house **(Reproducible 9A)**. This will make two houses. Let the children work together to decorate the house pages with crayons or markers.

Fold each house page along the dotted lines. Tape two house pages together to make a three-dimensional rectangle with no roof (see illustration). Cut one piece of **sandpaper** into two-inch strips. Lay the strips over the top of each house to make a roof. Place the houses in your story area.

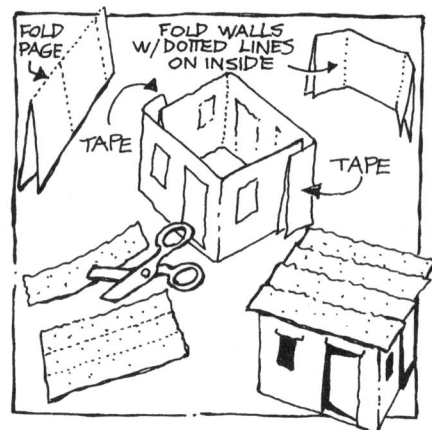

Say: Today our Bible story is about Jesus, four friends, and a man who could not walk. The four friends heard that Jesus was teaching in a house. The four friends wanted Jesus to help the man who could not walk. They carried the man to see Jesus. Jesus healed the man. Many people followed Jesus when they saw him make the man walk.

ZONE IN | **We can follow Jesus.**

Supplies:
construction paper, crayons

Zillies®:
smile face beanbag key chains

The Friendly Four

Have the children get in groups of four. (If you do not have the right number of children to do this, have the children get in groups of two or three.) Give each group a large piece of construction paper to make a Bible-times mat. Let the groups work together to decorate the mats with crayons.

Say: Today our Bible story is about Jesus, four friends, and a man who could not walk. The four friends carried the man to see Jesus. Let's pretend we are the four friends. We will take turns carrying our friend to see Jesus.

Choose two groups of children. Have all the children in each group hold their Bible-times mats. Place a **smile face beanbag key chain** on each mat. Let the children work together to carry the beanbags to your story area. Repeat the activity until all the groups have a turn.

108

BibleZone®

Bible ZONE

Hop 'n Stop

Supplies:
none

Zillies®:
none

Have the children line up behind you. Lead the children around the room as you say the verse printed below. Encourage the children to do the motions as you do. Have the children repeat the Bible verse after you each time. Lead the children to your story area.

Come, follow me
And hop, hop, hop,
(Hop around the room.)
Hop, hop, hop,
Hop, hop, hop.
Come, follow me
And hop, hop, hop.
Hop until I stop.
(Stop.)

Come, *(name each child).*
Jesus said, "Come, follow me."
(Motion "come here" with your arm.)

Come, follow me
And march, march, march,
(March around the room.)
March, march, march,
March, march, march.
Come, follow me
And march, march, march.
March until I stop.
(Stop.)

Come, *(name each child).*
Jesus said, "Come, follow me."
(Motion "come here" with your arm.)

Come, follow me
And tip-tiptoe,
(Tiptoe around the room.)
Tip-tiptoe,
Tip-tiptoe.
Come, follow me
And tip-tiptoe.
Tiptoe until I stop.
(Stop; have the children sit down in your story area.)

The Hole in the Roof

by Daphna Flegal

Have the children sit in a circle on the floor. Sit in the circle with the children. Place one of the Bible-times houses **(Reproducible 9A)** with the **sandpaper** roof strips in front of you. Hold the **smile face beanbag key chains** in your lap. Follow the directions as you tell the children the story.

Jesus was teaching in a house. *(Point to the house.)* Many, many people had come to hear Jesus teach about God's love. The house was full of people. There were even people standing outside the house, trying to hear Jesus.

There was a man who could not walk. The man had four friends. The four friends wanted to help the man.

"Let's take our friend to see Jesus," said one of the four friends. "Jesus will make our friend walk again."

The four friends carried the man to the house where Jesus was teaching.

(Give the beanbag to the child sitting next to you. Have the children pass the beanbag around the circle. When the beanbag comes back to you, hold it where the children can see it.)

The four friends tried to take the man into the house.

(Give the beanbag to the child sitting next to you. Have the children pass the beanbag around the circle. When the beanbag comes back to you, hold it where the children can see it.)

But the four friends could not get the man into the house. There were too many people. So the four friends decided to take the man up to the roof.

(Give the beanbag to the child sitting next to you. Have the children pass the beanbag around the circle. When the beanbag comes back to you, hold it where the children can see it.)

The four friends made a hole in the roof. *(Take off the sandpaper strips.)* They tied ropes to each corner of the man's mat. The four friends carefully lowered the man down through the hole to the floor right beside Jesus. *(Hold the beanbag by the key chain. Lower the beanbag into the house.)*

Jesus saw the man who could not walk. Jesus looked up and saw the four friends watching from the roof. Jesus looked back at the man lying on the floor.

"Stand up!" said Jesus. "Take up your mat and walk!"

(Pull the beanbag out of the house. Make the beanbag dance around.)

The man stood up! He started to walk!

(Give the beanbag to the child sitting next to you. Have the children pass the beanbag around the circle. When the beanbag comes back to you, hold it where the children can see it.)

"Praise God!" said the people. They were surprised that Jesus made the man walk. Many people became followers of Jesus.

Bible Verse Buzz

Choose a child to hold the Bible open to Mark 1:17.

Say: Today our Bible story is about when Jesus healed a man who could not walk. Many people followed Jesus when they saw him make the man walk.

Say the Bible verse, "And Jesus said to them, 'Follow me'" (Mark 1:17), for the children. Have the children say the Bible verse after you.

Turn your back to the children or hide your hands underneath a table or behind the **BibleZone® FUNspirational® Kit** lid as you place the **BZ Bee puppet** (see page 174) on your hand. Turn around or bring the puppet out where the children can see it.

Pretend to make the puppet talk. Change your voice for the puppet:

Bzzz. Bzzz. Bzzz. Hi, everybody! I'm BZ Bee. *Bzzz. Bzzz. Bzzz.* I like to taste fingers. Do you have fingers? Yum, yum, yum. Let me taste.

Go to each child. Encourage, but do not force, each child to hold up his or her fingers. Have BZ pretend to taste each child's fingers. Have BZ say things like:

Mmmm. Mmmm. You taste like honey. *Bzzz. Bzzz.* You taste like strawberries. *Yumm. Yumm.* You taste like blueberries.

After BZ has tasted each child's fingers, say:

Bzzz. Bzzz. Bzzz. I like to taste your fingers. They're yummy. *(Rub BZ's stomach.)*

Bzzz. Bzzz. Bzzz. I like something else even more than fingers.

I like the Bible. *Bzzz. Bzzz. Bzzz.* You heard a Bible story today. Who was the man in the story? *(Jesus)* What did the four friends do for the man who could not walk? *(took him to Jesus, lowered him through the roof)* What did Jesus do when he saw the man? *(made him walk)*

Bzzz. Bzzz. Bzzz. Many people followed Jesus when they saw him make the man walk.

Zone In: We can follow Jesus.

Bzzz. Bzzz. Bzzz. Let's all say the Bible verse together.

"And Jesus said to them, 'Follow me'" (Mark 1:17).

Have the children repeat the Bible verse with BZ Bee.

Have BZ Bee say goodbye to the children.

Bible Z⊙NE®

Choose one or more activities to immerse your children in the Bible story.

Supplies:
cassette player

Zillies®:
Cassette

Sing!

Have the children sit down. Play the song "Stand Up For Jesus" from the **Cassette.** Have the children stand up each time they hear the phrase, "Stand up for Jesus."

Stand Up For Jesus

Stand up for Jesus,
praise Him with a shout,
"Hey!" Ev'rybody, now sing glory hallelujah!
For He will be your everlasting friend
When you ask Him in your heart.

Lift your voices to the sky yi!
For He is forevermore the Lord most high!
Clap your hands, rejoice and sing,
For we belong to the King!

Stand up for Jesus,
praise Him with a shout,
"Hey!" Ev'rybody, now sing glory hallelujah!
For He will be your everlasting friend
When you ask Him in your heart.

Ev'rybody stand up for Jesus!

Writers: Jan Esterline, Janet McMahan Wilson, Ted Wilson

© 1990 New Spring Publishing, Inc. (ASCAP)/Bridge Building Music, Inc. (BMI) (both admin. by Brentwood-Benson Music Publishing, Inc.) All Rights Reserved. Used by Permission.

From the Brentwood-Benson Music Publishing, Inc. recording, *Kids Sing Praise, Vol. 3.*

Life Zone

Choose one or more activities to bring the Bible to life.

House Hop

(P)lace both Bible-times houses (**Reproducible 9A**) on one side of the room. Lay the **sandpaper** strips over the top of each house to make a roof (see page 108). Place a **smile face beanbag key chain** beside each house.

Say: **The four friends carried the man who could not walk to see Jesus. When they saw all the people, they carried the man up to the roof. They made a hole in the roof and lowered the man through the hole to Jesus. Let's pretend that we are the four friends. Let's lower the man through the roof.**

Have the children find a friend and move to the other side of the room. Call two pairs of children at a time.

Say: **Friend** (*child's name*) **and Friend** (*child's name*), **Friend** (*child's name*) **and Friend** (*child's name*), **hop to the houses.**

Have the pairs of children hop to the paper houses. Have one child in each pair take off the roof strips from the houses. Have the other child in each pair hold the smile face beanbag by the key chain and lower the beanbag into the house. Then have the pairs hop back to the other side of the room.

Place the beanbags back beside the houses and replace the sandpaper strips for the roofs. Repeat the game until every child has had a turn.

Say: **Jesus healed the man who could not walk. Many people followed Jesus when they saw him make the man walk. We can follow Jesus.**

Supplies:
Reproducible 9A

Zillies®:
sandpaper, smile face beanbag key chains

Ankle Bracelets

(P)hotocopy and cut apart the Bible verse strips (**Reproducible 9B**). You will need two strips for each child.

Say: **Now let's pretend you are the man who could not walk. Sit down with your legs stretched out. Remember, you cannot move your legs.**

Go to each child and tape Bible verse strips around the child's ankles.

Say: (*Child's name*) **can follow Jesus. Stand up and walk.**

Encourage the children to move around the room. Vary the movement you give each child (*jump, tiptoe, march, gallop, dance*).

Supplies:
Reproducible 9B, scissors, tape

Zillies®:

Supplies:
none

Zillies®:
none

Bible Verse Sing-along

Have the children sit down in a circle on the floor.

Say: Today our Bible story is about when Jesus healed a man who could not walk. Many people followed Jesus when they saw him make the man walk.

Teach the children the song "Follow Me" to the tune of "Hot Cross Buns."

"Follow me."
"Follow me."
Jesus said to his disciples,
"Follow me."

© 1999 by Abingdon Press.

Supplies:
none

Zillies®:
none

Sign 'n Pray

Have the children sit in a circle on the floor. Teach the children the Bible verse in American Sign Language. Go around the circle and name each child.

Say: *(Child's name)*, Jesus said, "Come, follow me."

Have the child sign the verse with you.

Pray: Thank you, God, for the good news that you love *(name each child and teacher)*. Amen.

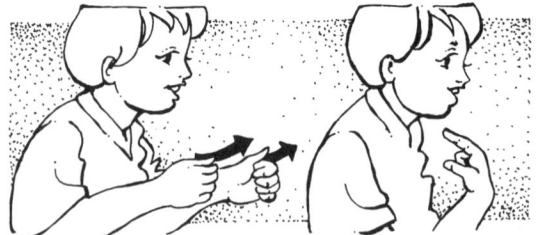

© 1998 Abingdon Press

Follow—Make a fist with both hands, thumbs out. Hold the right fist behind the left fist. Move both fists forward. Me—Point index finger of the right hand toward your chest.

Photocopy the **HomeZone**® newsletter to send home to parents.

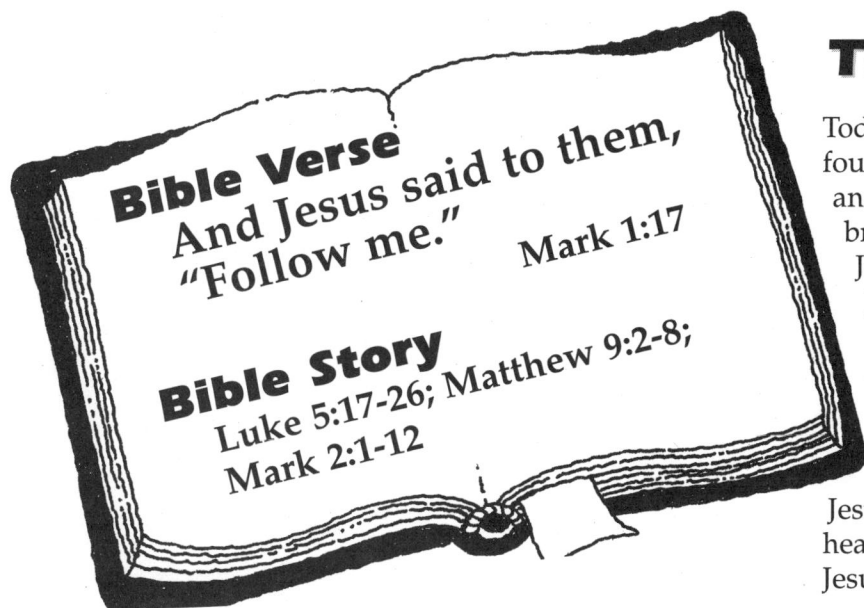

Through the Roof

Today your child heard the Bible story of four friends, a man who could not walk, and Jesus. The four friends wanted to bring the man who could not walk to Jesus so that he could heal the man. Jesus was teaching in a house, and there were so many people, the four friends could not get close to Jesus. So the friends carried the man up to the roof. They made a hole in the roof and lowered the man to Jesus. Jesus had compassion for the man and healed him. The people were amazed at Jesus and praised God.

Bible Verse
And Jesus said to them, "Follow me." Mark 1:17

Bible Story
Luke 5:17-26; Matthew 9:2-8; Mark 2:1-12

And Jesus said to them, "Follow me." Mark 1:17

Bible Verse Sing-along

Help your child remember the Bible verse with a song. Sing "Follow Me" to the tune of "Hot Cross Buns."

"Follow me."
"Follow me."
Jesus said to his disciples,
"Follow me."

© 1999 by Abingdon Press.

Remind your child that many people followed Jesus when they saw him heal people like the man who could not walk. We can read stories about Jesus from the Bible, and we can follow him.

We can follow Jesus.

Permission granted to photocopy for local church use. © 1999 Abingdon Press.

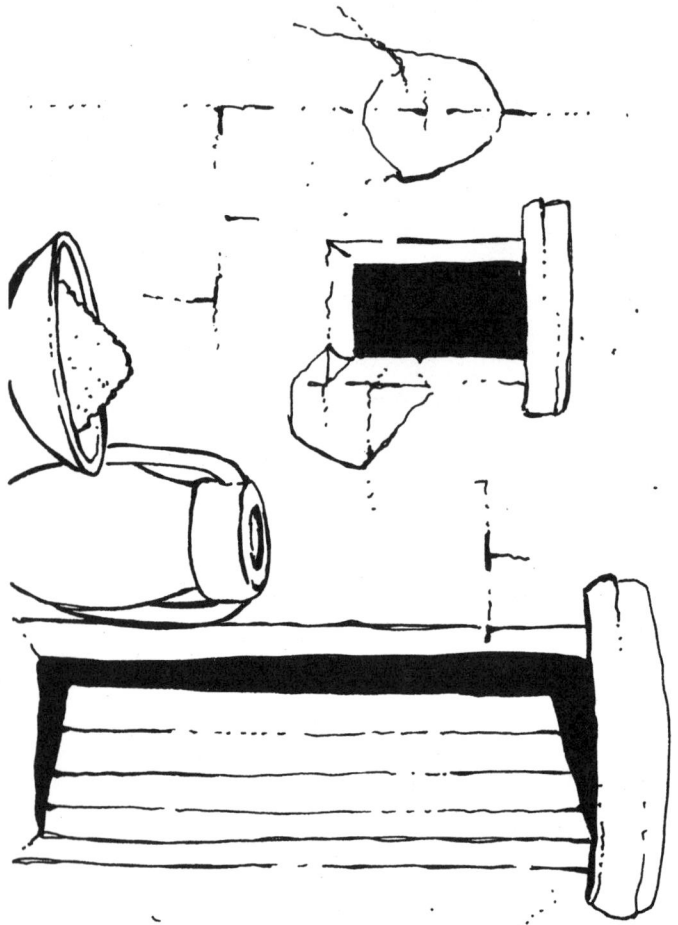
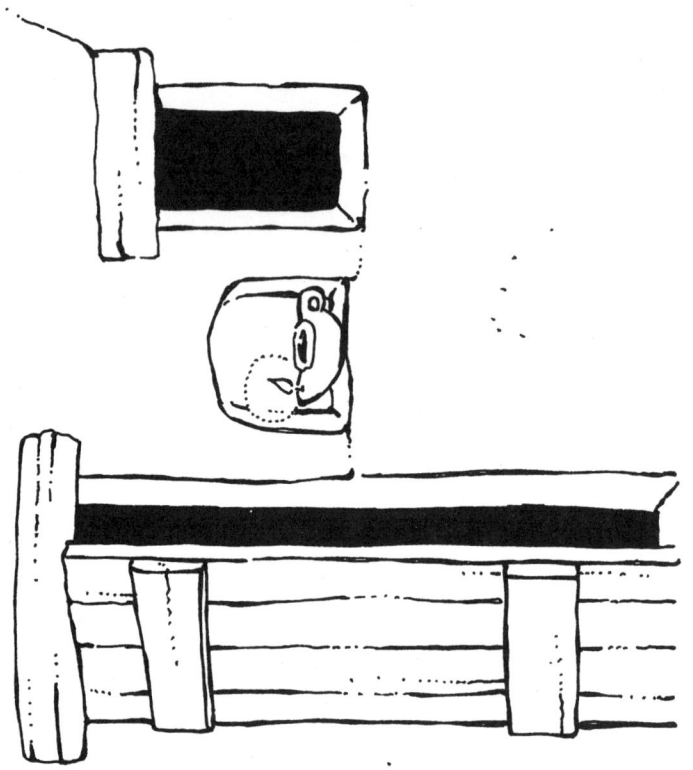
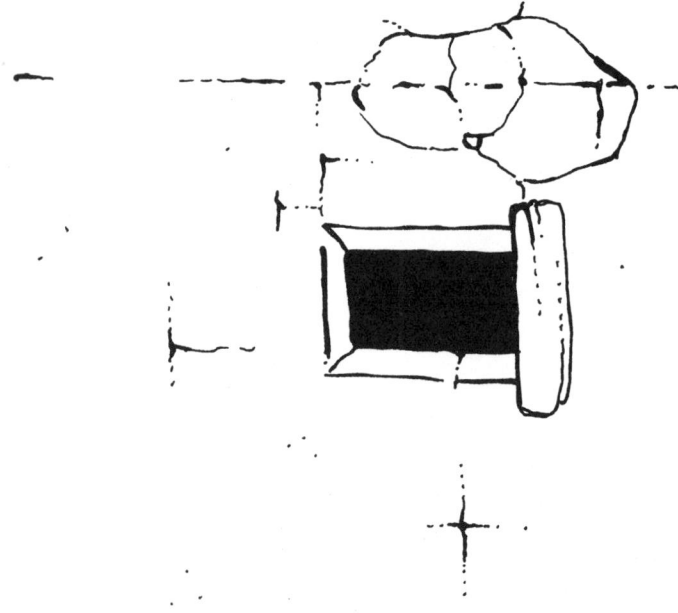
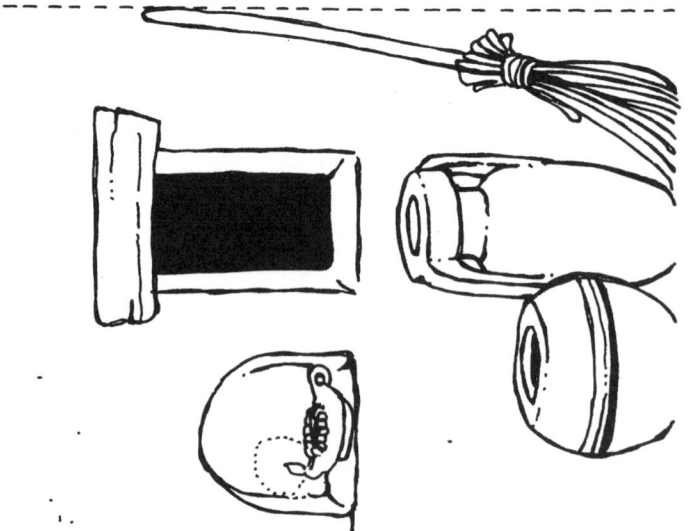

Reproducible 9A

BIBLEZONE®

And Jesus said to them, "Follow me." Mark 1:17

And Jesus said to them, "Follow me." Mark 1:17

And Jesus said to them, "Follow me." Mark 1:17

And Jesus said to them, "Follow me." Mark 1:17

Reproducible 9B

With His Friends

Enter the Zone

Bible Verse
And Jesus said to them, "Follow me."
Mark 1:17

Bible Story
Luke 10:38-42

Poor Martha, the busy hostess in the story of Jesus' visit to Mary and Martha, is often held up as a bad example. Then we spend most of our lives doing just what Martha did and for the very same reason.

Martha had a duty to serve her guests and to be hospitable. In the culture of her time, being hospitable was considered mandatory. Like Martha, we're all irritated from time to time by a Mary who doesn't do her share and is praised for it!

In this story Jesus was not chastising Martha for doing her duty or praising Mary for goofing off. Instead, he was showing us that, like Martha, we often miss the whole point.

Martha had done more than was required. She became distracted by her tasks and did not do the most important thing—listen to her guest. Mary, on the other hand, had figured out that enough had been done to meet the basic requirements of hospitality, and it was okay to take time to listen.

We too are often distracted by serving. We act as if the whole point is how much serving we can do. Sometimes we put our souls at risk while doing very worthwhile things. We fail to stop and listen to the Word of God and to be refreshed. The serving becomes an end in itself. Sometimes we don't do the right kind of serving because we have forgotten the message.

Many of us attempt to fill our lives with things and activities, hoping to find the meaning of life. We are disappointed when we still can't figure it out. If we were like Mary, we would sometimes stop and listen, and the meaning of life might be shown to us.

Most young children are eager learners when learning can be made into an enjoyable pastime. Children respond best to a combination of active and quiet activities. Listening is an important part of learning, and learning to listen is something that children must practice. Give your children many opportunities for both quiet and active activities. Affirm the importance of both and encourage the children to participate in both quiet and active play.

We can listen to Jesus' teachings and follow him.

Scope the ZONE

ZONE	TIME	SUPPLIES	⊚ ZILLIES®
Zoom Into the Zone			
Sister, Sister	10 minutes	Reproducible 10A; crayons or markers; tape, glue, or stapler and staples	none
Sisterly Sit Upons	10 minutes	Reproducible 10B; crayons; tape or stapler and staples; paper, tissues, or cotton balls	none
BibleZone®			
Hop 'n Stop	5 minutes	none	none
Mary and Martha	10 minutes	puppets and pillows (Reproducibles 10A and 10B)	none
Bible Verse Buzz	5 minutes	Bible, BZ Bee	none
Sing!	5 minutes	cassette player	Cassette
LifeZone			
Listening Lessons	10 minutes	pillows (Reproducible 10B)	celestial ball
Bible Verse Sing-along	5 minutes	none	none
Sign 'n Pray	5 minutes	none	none

⊚ Zillies® are found in the **BibleZone® FUNspirational® Kit.**

Zoom Into the Zone

Supplies:
Reproducible 10A; crayons or markers; tape, glue, or stapler and staples

Zillies®:
none

Sister, Sister

Photocopy the Mary and Martha figures **(Reproducible 10A)** for each child. Let the children decorate the figures with crayons or markers. Show the children how to fold their pages along the dotted lines. Let the children tape, glue, or staple the edges of the figures together, leaving the bottoms open. Show the children how to put their hands in the opening at the bottom to make puppets.

Say: **Today our Bible story is about Jesus and two of his friends, Mary and Martha. Mary and Martha were sisters. Martha was very busy.** *(Turn the puppet to the picture of Martha sweeping.)* **Mary sat and listened to Jesus.** *(Turn the puppet to the picture of Mary sitting.)*

ZONE IN: **We can listen to Jesus' teachings and follow him.**

Write the children's names on their puppets. Place the puppets in your story area.

Supplies:
Reproducible 10B; crayons; tape or stapler and staples; paper, tissues, or cotton balls

Zillies®:
none

Sisterly Sit Upons

Photocopy two copies of the flower pictures **(Reproducible 10B)** for each child. Let the children make pillows. Have the children decorate the flowers with crayons.

Help each child place the two papers together so that the decorated flowers face out. Staple or tape three sides of the papers together. Show the children how to stuff the the pillows with crumpled paper, tissues, or cotton balls. Tape or staple the remaining sides together.

Say: **Today our Bible story is about Jesus and two of his friends, Mary and Martha. Mary and Martha were sisters. Martha was very busy. Mary sat and listened to Jesus. We will use our pillows to sit and listen to a Bible story about Jesus and his friends.**

Have the children place their pillows on the floor in your story area.

Bible ZONE

Choose one or more activities to immerse your children in the Bible story.

Hop 'n Stop

Supplies:
none

Zillies®:
none

(H)ave the children line up behind you. Lead the children around the room as you say the verse printed below. Encourage the children to do the motions as you do. Have the children repeat the Bible verse after you each time. Lead the children to your story area.

Come, follow me
And hop, hop, hop,
(Hop around the room.)
Hop, hop, hop,
Hop, hop, hop.
Come, follow me
And hop, hop, hop.
Hop until I stop.
(Stop.)

Come, *(name each child)*.
Jesus said, "Come, follow me."
(Motion "come here" with your arm.)

Come, follow me
And march, march, march,
(March around the room.)
March, march, march,
March, march, march.
Come, follow me
And march, march, march.
March until I stop.
(Stop.)

Come, *(name each child)*.
Jesus said, "Come, follow me."
(Motion "come here" with your arm.)

Come, follow me
And tip-tiptoe,
(Tip toe around the room.)
Tip-tiptoe,
Tip-tiptoe.
Come, follow me
And tip-tiptoe,
Tiptoe until I stop.
(Stop; have the children sit down in your story area.)

Mary and Martha

by Daphna Flegal

*H*ave the children sit on their pillows **(Reproducible 10B)** in your story area. Give each child her or his puppet **(Reproducible 10A)**. Show the children how to turn the puppets to the side with the picture of Mary sitting, then to the side with the picture of Martha sweeping.

*Say: I want you to help me tell the Bible story. When I say the name **Mary**, turn your puppets to the side with Mary sitting. She is sitting, listening to Jesus teach about God. When I say the name **Martha**, turn your puppets to the side with Martha sweeping. She is very busy cleaning and cooking.*

Mary and **Martha** were sisters. They followed Jesus.

One day Jesus came to **Mary** and **Martha's** house.

Mary and **Martha** were very excited to see Jesus. He was their friend.

Martha was very busy. She cleaned the house from top to bottom. She cooked a meal for Jesus. She worked and worked.

Mary was not busy. She sat by Jesus. She listened to him teach about God's love.

Martha became upset! She wanted someone to help her with all the work.

"Jesus," **Martha** said. "I am so busy. Tell **Mary** to help me."

"**Martha, Martha,**" answered Jesus. "All the work you are doing can wait. Come, sit down and listen. **Mary** is learning about God."

Martha wanted to learn about God. She sat down beside **Mary** and listened to Jesus.

Mary and **Martha** listened to Jesus' teachings and followed him.

Sing the song printed below with the children to the tune of "Twinkle, Twinkle, Little Star." Have the children begin by turning their puppets to the Martha picture.

Say: Let's pretend Martha is singing this part of the song.

> Mary, Mary, where are you?
> I've got so much work to do.
> Come and help me cook and clean.
> If you don't, I'll think you're mean.
> Mary, Mary, where are you?
> I've got so much work to do.

Say: Let's pretend Jesus is singing this part of the song.

> Martha, Martha, listen well.
> Hear the things I have to tell.
> Mary's doing the right thing,
> Listening to the news I bring.
> Martha, Martha, listen well.
> Hear the things I have to tell.

Words: Daphna Flegal and Linda Ray Miller.
© 1997 Abingdon Press.

Bible Verse Buzz

Choose a child to hold the Bible open to Mark 1:17.

Say: Today our Bible story is about Jesus and two of his friends, Mary and Martha. Mary and Martha were sisters. They were followers of Jesus.

Say the Bible verse, "And Jesus said to them, 'Follow me'" (Mark 1:17), for the children. Have the children say the Bible verse after you.

Turn your back to the children or hide your hands underneath a table or behind the **BibleZone® FUNspirational® Kit** lid as you place the **BZ Bee puppet** (see page 174) on your hand. Turn around or bring the puppet out where the children can see it.

Pretend to make the puppet talk. Change your voice for the puppet:

Bzzz. Bzzz. Bzzz. Hi, everybody! I'm BZ Bee. *Bzzz. Bzzz. Bzzz.* I like to taste fingers. Do you have fingers? Yum, yum, yum. Let me taste.

Go to each child. Encourage, but do not force, each child to hold up his or her fingers. Have BZ pretend to taste each child's fingers. Have BZ say things like:

Mmmm. Mmmm. You taste like honey. *Bzzz. Bzzz.* You taste like strawberries. *Yumm. Yumm.* You taste like blueberries.

After BZ has tasted each child's fingers, say:

Bzzz. Bzzz. Bzzz. I like to taste your fingers. They're yummy. *(Rub BZ's stomach.)*

Bzzz. Bzzz. Bzzz. I like something else even more than fingers.

I like the Bible. *Bzzz. Bzzz. Bzzz.* You heard a Bible story today. Who was the man in the story? *(Jesus)* Who were the two women in today's story? *(Mary and Martha)* What was Martha doing? *(She was busy getting ready for Jesus.)* What was Mary doing? *(She was listening to Jesus.)*

Bzzz. Bzzz. Bzzz. Mary and Martha listened to Jesus' teachings and followed him.

> **We can listen to Jesus' teachings and follow him.**

Bzzz. Bzzz. Bzzz. Let's all say the Bible verse together.

"And Jesus said to them, 'Follow me'" (Mark 1:17).

Have the children repeat the Bible verse with BZ Bee.

Have BZ Bee say goodbye to the children.

Bible ZONE

Choose one or more activities to immerse your children in the Bible story.

Supplies:
cassette player

Zillies®:
Cassette

Sing!

(P) lay the song "Happy All the Time" from the **Cassette** and do the suggested motions with the children.

Inright—both hands point to self.
Outright—both hands point out.
Upright—both hands point to ceiling.
Downright—both hands point down.

Happy All the Time

I'm inright, outright, upright, downright,
happy all the time,
I'm inright, outright, upright, downright,
happy all the time.
Since Jesus Christ came in
and cleansed my heart from sin,
I'm inright, outright, upright, downright,
happy all the time.

I'm inright, outright, upright, downright,
happy all the time,
I'm inright, outright, upright, downright,
happy all the time.
Since Jesus Christ came in
and cleansed my heart from sin,
I'm inright, outright, upright, downright,
happy all the time.

I'm inright, outright, upright, downright,
happy all the time,
I'm inright, outright, upright, downright,
happy all the time.
Since Jesus Christ came in
and cleansed my heart from sin,
I'm inright, outright, upright, downright,
happy all the time.

I'm inright, outright, upright, downright,
happy all the time.

Choose one or more activities to bring the Bible to life.

Listening Lessons

Have the children bring their pillows **(Reproducible 10B)** and move to an open area in the room.

Say: Today our Bible story is about Jesus and two of his friends, Mary and Martha. Mary and Martha were sisters. Martha was very busy. Mary sat and listened to Jesus. Let's play a listening game. You will need to listen very carefully and do what I tell you to do.

Use the suggestions printed below to play a listening game with the children.

Put your pillows on the floor.
Touch one hand to your pillows.
Touch your elbow to your pillows.
Hop in a circle around your pillows.
Touch your ear to your pillows.
Lie down with your head on your pillows.
Close your eyes.
Listen very carefully. *(Bounce the celestial ball on the floor or on a table top.)*
What do you hear? *(Let the children guess that they hear a ball bouncing.)*
Open your eyes.
Sit up.
You are good listeners. Let's play a clapping game. I will clap a pattern, and you will listen and repeat it after me. Listen carefully so you will know exactly what I do.

Use simple patterns and work slowly with the children. Vary the clapping between soft and loud. Include patting your knees, your head, and the floor.

Say: Mary and Martha listened to Jesus' teachings and followed him.

ZONE IN
We can listen to Jesus' teachings and follow him.

Life Zone ®

Choose one or more activities to bring the Bible to life.

Supplies:
none

Zillies®:
none

Bible Verse Sing-a-long

Have the children sit down in a circle on the floor.

Say: Today our Bible story is about Jesus and two of his friends, Mary and Martha. Mary and Martha were sisters. They were followers of Jesus.

Teach the children the song "Follow Me" to the tune of "Hot Cross Buns."

"Follow me."
"Follow me."
Jesus said to his disciples,
"Follow me."

© 1999 by Abingdon Press.

Supplies:
none

Zillies®:
none

Sign 'n Pray

Have the children sit in a circle on the floor. Teach the children the Bible verse in American Sign Language. Go around the circle and name each child.

Say: (*Child's name*), Jesus said, "Come, follow me."

Have the child sign the verse with you.

Pray: Thank you, God, for the good news that you love (*name each child and teacher*). Amen.

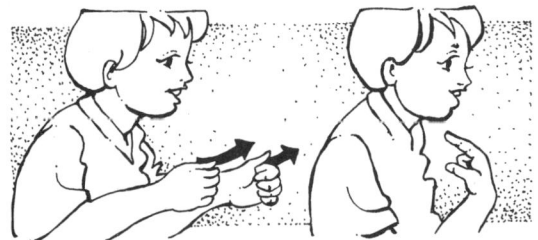

© 1998 Abingdon Press

Follow—Make a fist with both hands, thumbs out. Hold the right fist behind the left fist. Move both fists forward. Me—Point index finger of the right hand toward your chest.

Photocopy the **HomeZone**® newsletter to send home to parents.

Home ZONE For Parents

With His Friends

Today your child heard the Bible story of Jesus and his friends, Mary and Martha. Martha spent her time working to get ready for Jesus. Mary spent her time at Jesus' feet, listening to him teach about God. Jesus helped Martha learned that sometimes it is important to put aside your work and learn about God.

Bible Verse
And Jesus said to them, "Follow me."   Mark 1:17

Bible Story
Luke 10:38-42

Sing a Story Song

Help your child remember the story of Mary and Martha with a song. Sing the words printed below to the tune of "Twinkle, Twinkle, Little Star."

Mary, Mary, where are you?
I've got so much work to do.
Come and help me cook and clean.
If you don't, I'll think you're mean.
Mary, Mary, where are you?
I've got so much work to do.

Martha, Martha, listen well.
Hear the things I have to tell.
Mary's doing the right thing,
Listening to the news I bring.
Martha, Martha, listen well.
Hear the things I have to tell.

Words: Daphna Flegal and Linda Ray Miller.
© 1997 Abingdon Press.

ZONE IN

We can listen to Jesus' teachings and follow him.

PRESCHOOL   10   Permission granted to photocopy for local church use. © 1999 Abingdon Press.   127

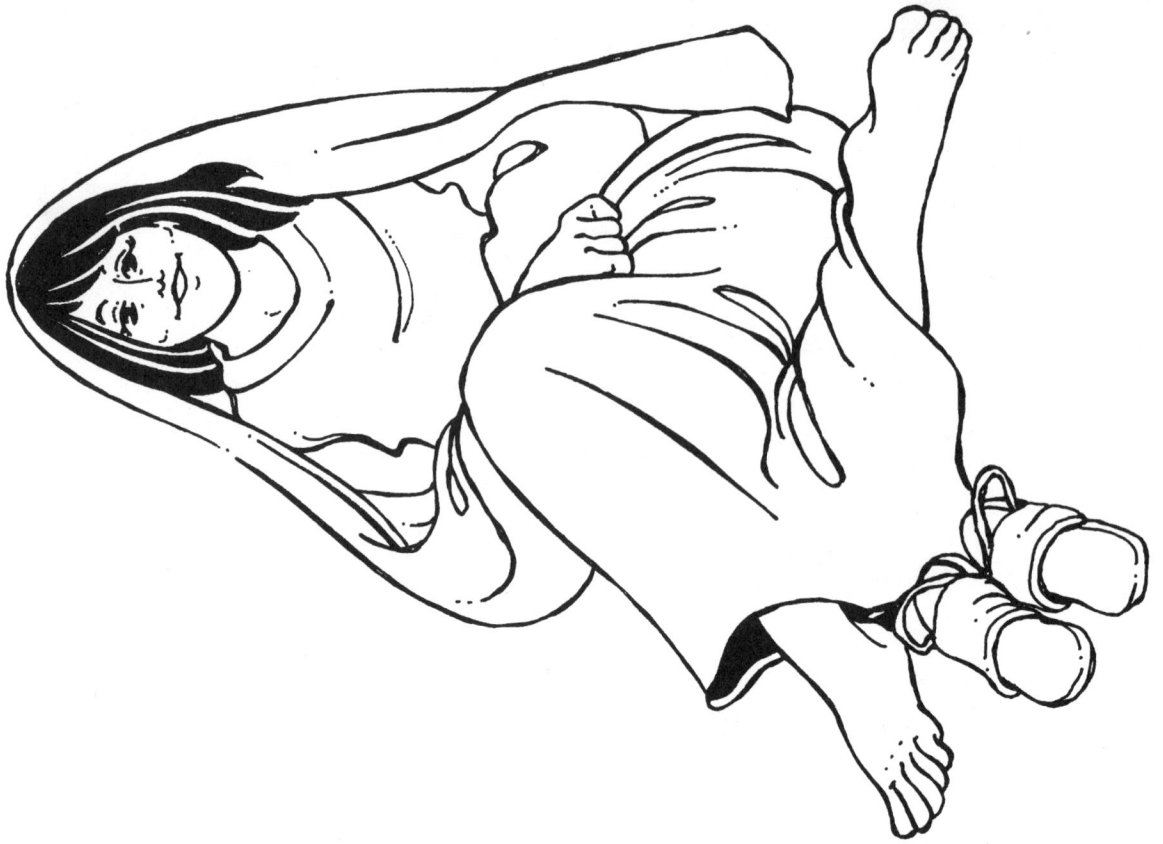

Reproducible 10A

BIBLEZONE®

Reproducible 10B

Out of the Tomb

Enter the ZONE

Bible Verse
Sing for joy to the LORD.
Psalm 98:4, *Good News Bible*

Bible Story
Matthew 27:32–28:10

The Resurrection story is not only a story of joy, hope, and new life, but it is also the account of the event around which all Christianity is built. The story tells of the women who arrived at the tomb at dawn on Sunday morning to prepare the body. With the sabbath beginning at sundown on Friday, there had only been time to place Jesus' body in the tomb. Any preparation of the dead would have had to wait until after the sabbath, or the first day of the week.

Matthew describes the tomb. The tomb was was carved out of rock. The Bible tells us that it was a new tomb that Joseph of Arimathea had cut out of stone for himself. It was likely sealed with a large, round stone that rolled in a groove in front of the cave-like tomb opening. There was a great earthquake, and an angel rolled back the stone.

It is not surprising that the women who saw this event were filled with fear. The angel told the women at the tomb not to be afraid. Then the angel told the women that Jesus was not in the tomb. Jesus was alive! The women left the tomb, filled with joy. The experience at the tomb of the risen

Christ on the first day of the week was the beginning of the Christian Sunday celebration of the Resurrection. The joy that the women felt at the empty tomb is also our joy. Let's sing for joy to the Lord!

Mary Magdalene and the other women discovered the empty tomb and encountered the risen Jesus. They were filled with awe and joy. Jesus told the women to spread the good news of the Resurrection to the disciples. Pray for God's help as you plan opportunities for young children to celebrate and to spread the joy of the Resurrection to others.

ZONE IN

We celebrate with joy because we know Jesus is alive!

Scope the ZONE

ZONE	TIME	SUPPLIES	⊚ ZILLIES®
Zoom Into the Zone			
Big Rock Surprise	10 minutes	Reproducible 11A, crayons or markers, gray or brown construction paper or tissue paper, glue	none
Kites of Joy	10 minutes	Reproducible 11B, newspapers or mural paper, tape, cassette player, crayons or markers, paper punch, scissors	ribbon, Cassette
BibleZone®			
Going to the Tomb	5 minutes	none	none
Joy! Joy! Joy	10 minutes	none	none
Bible Verse Buzz	5 minutes	Bible, BZ Bee	none
Sing!	5 minutes	kites (Reproducible 11B), cassette player	Cassette
LifeZone			
Touch Joy	10 minutes	Reproducible 11A, tape	none
Where Is Happy?	5 minutes	none	smile face finger puppets
Sign 'n Pray	5 minutes	none	none

⊚ Zillies® are found in the **BibleZone® FUNspirational® Kit.**

PRESCHOOL 10

131

Zoom Into the Zone

Choose one or more activities to catch your children's interest.

Supplies:
Reproducible 11A, crayons or markers, gray or brown construction paper or tissue paper, glue

Zillies®:
none

Big Rock Surprise

Photocopy the picture of the garden tomb **(Reproducible 11A)** for each child. Let the children color the pictures with crayons or markers.

Say: **Today our Bible story is very special. Jesus died and was buried in a tomb.** *(Point to the picture of the tomb.)* **The tomb was like a cave. Jesus' body was put in the tomb, and a big rock was rolled in front of the opening. Two women came to the tomb. They were sad because their friend Jesus was dead. But something happened when they got to the tomb. What do you see sitting on the big rock in our pictures?** *(an angel)* **The women saw an angel! The angel told the women that Jesus was not in the tomb. Jesus was alive! The women were no longer sad. They were happy and filled with joy!**

> **We celebrate with joy because we know Jesus is alive!**

Give each child a piece of gray or brown construction paper or tissue paper. Show the children how to crumple the paper into a ball. Have the children glue the crumpled paper onto the the big rock (that the angel is sitting on) in the picture. Lay the pictures flat for the glue to dry.

Supplies:
Reproducible 11B, newspapers or mural paper, tape, cassette player, crayons or markers, paper punch, scissors

Zillies®:
ribbon, Cassette

Kites of Joy

Photocopy the butterflies **(Reproducible 11B)** for each child. Cover a section of the wall that is easy for the children to reach with newspapers or mural paper. Lightly tape a butterfly picture for each child to the paper. Play the song "Ha-Le-La-Le-La-Le-Lu-Jah" from the **Cassette**.

Have the children stand in front of their papers. Let the children decorate the butterflies with crayons or markers as the music plays.

Say: **Today our Bible story is filled with joy. Let's listen to happy, joyful music and let your hands "dance" the colors onto your pictures.**

Show the children how to fold their butterflies in half. Use a paper punch to punch a hole in the top of each picture. Tie a piece of **ribbon** through each hole to make a handle. Show the children how to wave their butterflies in the air.

Bible ZONE

Choose one or more activities to immerse your children in the Bible story.

Going to the Tomb

Supplies:
none

Zillies®:
none

Have the children move to an open area of the room.

Say: Jesus died and was buried in a tomb. Two women came to the tomb. They were sad. Show me how you look when you are sad. *(Let the children make sad faces.)* **But something happened when they got to the tomb. The women saw an angel! The women were surprised. Show me how you look when you're surprised.** *(Encourage the children to look surprised.)* **The angel told the women that Jesus was not in the tomb. Jesus was alive! The women were happy. Show me how you look when you are happy.** *(Encourage the children to look happy.)*

Sing the song printed below to the tune of "This Is the Way" and do the motions with the children.

> This is the way the women walked,
> *(Walk in place.)*
> Women walked, women walked.
> This is the way the women walked,
> Going to the tomb.
>
> This is the way the women looked,
> *(Look surprised.)*
> Women looked, women looked.
> This is the way the women looked
> Inside the tomb.
>
> This is the way the women ran,
> *(Run in place.)*
> Women ran, women ran.
> This is the way the women ran
> To tell the good news.

Words: Linda Ray Miller
© 1997 Abingdon Press.

ZONE IN **We celebrate with joy because we know Jesus is alive!**

Joy! Joy! Joy!

by Daphna Flegal

Have the children stand in a circle in your story area. Tell the children the story. Encourage the children to say the repeated words after you and to do the suggested motions. After you tell the story, repeat the words and motions with the children to help them remember the story.

Walk. Walk. Walk. *(Walk in place.)* Two women walked to the garden. It was very early in the morning. The sun was just beginning to shine.

Cry. Cry. Cry. *(Pretend to rub eyes.)* The two women were very sad. Their friend, Jesus, was dead. He was buried in the garden tomb. A big rock was in front of the tomb.

Shake. Shake. Shake. *(Shake hands in front of your body.)* Suddenly the ground began to shake. It was an earthquake! The two women saw an angel come down from the sky. The angel was bright with light.

"Oh! Oh! Oh!" *(Put hands on either side of your face.)* The women were afraid. They watched the angel roll the big rock away from the door of the tomb. The women watched as the angel sat on the big rock.

"No. No. No," *(Shake head no.)* said the angel. "Do not be afraid. I know you are looking for Jesus. Come and see the inside of the tomb. He is not here. He is alive!"

"Go. Go. Go," *(Point away from yourself.)* said the angel. "Go and tell his friends, 'Jesus is alive!'"

Run. Run. Run. *(Run in place.)* The women ran to tell Jesus' friends the good news. Jesus was alive!

Joy! Joy! Joy! *(Hold arms above your head and shake hands.)* The women were no longer sad. They were filled with joy because they knew Jesus was alive!

Walk. Walk. Walk.
(Walk in place.)
Cry. Cry. Cry.
(Pretend to rub eyes.)
Shake. Shake. Shake.
(Shake hands in front of your body.)
"Oh! Oh! Oh!"
(Put hands on either side of your face.)
"No. No. No."
(Shake head no.)
"Go. Go. Go."
(Point away from yourself.)
Run. Run. Run.
(Run in place.)
Joy! Joy! Joy!
(Hold arms above your head and shake hands.)

Bible Verse Buzz

Choose a child to hold the Bible open to Psalm 98:4.

Say: Today our Bible story is very special. Jesus died and was buried in a tomb. Two women came to the tomb. They were sad because their friend Jesus was dead. But something happened when they got to the tomb. The women saw an angel! The angel told the women that Jesus was not in the tomb. Jesus was alive! The women were happy and filled with joy!

Say the Bible verse, "Sing for joy to the LORD" (Psalm 98:4, *Good News Bible*), for the children. Have the children say the Bible verse after you.

Turn your back to the children or hide your hands underneath a table or behind the **BibleZone® FUNspirational® Kit** lid as you place the **BZ Bee puppet** (see page 174) on your hand. Turn around or bring the puppet out where the children can see it.

Pretend to make the puppet talk. Change your voice for the puppet:

Bzzz. Bzzz. Bzzz. Hi, everybody! I'm BZ Bee. *Bzzz. Bzzz. Bzzz.* I like to taste fingers. Do you have fingers? Yum, yum, yum. Let me taste.

Go to each child. Encourage, but do not force, each child to hold up his or her fingers. Have BZ pretend to taste each child's fingers. Have BZ say things like:

Mmmm. Mmmm. You taste like honey. *Bzzz. Bzzz.* You taste like strawberries. *Yumm. Yumm.* You taste like blueberries.

After BZ has tasted each child's fingers, say:

Bzzz. Bzzz. Bzzz. I like to taste your fingers. They're yummy. *(Rub BZ's stomach.)*

Bzzz. Bzzz. Bzzz. I like something else even more than fingers.

I like the Bible. *Bzzz. Bzzz. Bzzz.* You heard a Bible story today. Who was buried in the tomb? *(Jesus)* Who went to see the tomb? *(two women)* What did the women see that surprised them? *(an angel)* What did the angel tell the women? *(Jesus was alive.)*

Bzzz. Bzzz. Bzzz. When the angel told the women that Jesus was alive, the women were happy and filled with joy.

We celebrate with joy because we know Jesus is alive!

Bzzz. Bzzz. Bzzz. Let's all say the Bible verse together.

"Sing for joy to the LORD" (Psalm 98:4, *Good News Bible*).

Have the children repeat the Bible verse with BZ Bee.

Have BZ Bee say goodbye to the children.

Choose one or more activities to immerse your children in the Bible story.

Supplies:
kites (Reproducible 11B), cassette player

Zillies®:
Cassette

Sing!

Have the children bring their kites (**Reproducible 11B**) and move to an open area of the room.

Say: When the angel told the women that Jesus was alive, the women were happy and filled with joy.

We celebrate with joy because we know Jesus is alive!

Play the song "Ha-Le-La-Le-La-Le-Lu-Jah" from the **Cassette**. Let the children dance and move with their kites as the music plays.

Ha-Le-La-Le-La-Le-Lu-Jah

Hal-le-la-le-la-le-lu-jah,
Hal-le-lu-jah to the Lord,
Hal-le-la-le-la-le-lu-jah,
Praise His name forevermore.
Hal-le-la-le-la-le-lu-jah,
Lift your voice, rejoice and sing
Hal-le-la-le-la-le-lu-jah,
to the King of Kings!

He is the Holy One,
Jesus, God's only Son,
crowning glory of all creation,
clap your hands in celebration!

Hal-le-la-le-la-le-lu-jah,
Hal-le-lu-jah to the Lord,
Hal-le-la-le-la-le-lu-jah,
Praise His name forevermore.
Hal-le-la-le-la-le-lu-jah,
Lift your voice, rejoice and sing
Hal-le-la-le-la-le-lu-jah,
to the King of Kings!

He is the Holy One,
Jesus, God's only Son,
crowning glory of all creation,
clap your hands in celebration!

Hal-le-la-le-la-le-lu-jah,
Hal-le-lu-jah to the Lord,
Hal-le-la-le-la-le-lu-jah,
Praise His name forevermore.
Hal-le-la-le-la-le-lu-jah,
Lift your voice, rejoice and sing
Hal-le-la-le-la-le-lu-jah,
to the King of Kings!

Hal-le-la-le-la-le-lu-jah,
to the King of Kings!

Writers: Janet McMahan-Wilson and Ted Wilson

Life Zone

Choose one or more activities to bring the Bible to life.

Touch Joy

Supplies:
Reproducible 11A, tape

Zillies®:
none

(P) hotocopy several copies of the garden tomb picture (**Reproducible 11A**). Tape the copies around your room. You might tape the pictures on the walls, in the center of tables, on the backs of chairs, and on the floor. Have the children sit down in the middle of the floor.

Say: **Today our Bible story is very special. Jesus died and was buried in a tomb. Two women came to the tomb. They were sad because their friend Jesus was dead. But something happened when they got to the tomb. The women saw an angel! The angel told the women that Jesus was not in the tomb. Jesus was alive! The women were happy and filled with joy!**

We celebrate with joy because we know Jesus is alive!

Say: **I will name a color or a thing that is in our room. When you hear me name something, get up and touch whatever it is that I named. Then sit back down. When I say, "Touch joy!", get up and find one of our garden pictures. Touch the picture and say the Bible verse, "Sing for joy to the LORD" (Psalm 98: 4, *Good News Bible*). Then sit back down.**

Use the suggestions below for the game. Help the children find the pictures to touch and say the Bible verse each time you say, "Touch joy!"

> **Touch a chair.**
> **Touch blue.**
> **Touch joy!**
> **Touch green.**
> **Touch joy!**
> **Touch a table.**
> **Touch purple.**
> **Touch red.**
> **Touch joy!**
> **Touch a friend.**
> **Touch joy!**

Life Zone

Choose one or more activities to bring the Bible to life.

Supplies:
none

Zillies®:
smile face finger puppets

Where Is Happy?

Have the children sit in a circle. Give each child two **smile face finger puppets.** Help each child put a finger puppet on each thumb. Lead the children in the fingerplay song below to the tune of "Are You Sleeping?"

Where is Happy?
(Put finger puppets behind your back.)
Where is Happy?
(Put finger puppets behind your back.)
Here I am!
(Bring one finger puppet to the front.)
Here I am!
(Bring second finger puppet to the front.)

Listen to God's Word now.
(Bend one finger puppet.)
Listen to God's Word now.
(Bend second finger puppet.)
Sing for joy
(Hold one finger puppet to ear.)
To the LORD!
(Hold second finger puppet to other ear.)

Supplies:
none

Zillies®:
none

Sing—Hold the left hand out. Point the right-hand fingers toward the left palm. Wave the fingertips back and forth over the left palm.

Joy—Open both hands, palms facing toward the chest. Pat the chest several times while moving the hands upwards.

Lord—Make an "L" with the right hand. Place the "L" at the left shoulder and then move across the body to the right waist.

Sign 'n Pray

Have the children sit in a circle on the floor. Teach the children the Bible verse in American Sign Language. Go around the circle and name each child.

© 1998 Abingdon Press

Say: *(Child's name)*, **sing for joy to the LORD.**

Have the child sign the verse with you.

Pray: Thank you, God, for the good news that Jesus is alive. Amen.

Photocopy the **HomeZone®** newsletter to send home to parents.

138

Bible Verse
Sing for joy to the LORD.
Psalm 98:4, *Good News Bible*

Bible Story
Matthew 27:32–28:10

Out of the Tomb

Today your child heard the story of Jesus' resurrection based on the Gospel of Matthew. Mary Magdalene and the other Mary went to the tomb early in the morning on the first day of the week. They wanted to prepare Jesus' body for burial. When the two women arrived at the tomb, there was a great earthquake, and an angel rolled back the stone. The women were filled with fear.

The angel told the women at the tomb not to be afraid. Then the angel told the women that Jesus was not in the tomb. Jesus was alive! The women left the tomb, filled with joy.

The experience at the tomb of the risen Christ on the first day of the week was the beginning of the Christian Sunday celebration of the Resurrection. The joy that the women felt at the empty tomb is also our joy. Let's sing for joy to the Lord!

Sign 'n Pray

Learn with your child the Bible verse, "Sing for joy to the LORD" (Psalm 98:4, *Good News Bible*), in American Sign Language.

Sing—Hold the left hand out. Point the fingers of the right hand toward the left palm. Wave the fingertips back and forth over the left palm.

Joy—Open both hands, with palms facing toward the chest. Pat the chest several times while moving the hands upwards.

Lord—Make an "L" with the right hand. Place the "L" at the left shoulder and then move across the body to the right waist.

sing   joy   Lord

We celebrate with joy because we know Jesus is alive!

Reproducible 11A

BIBLEZONE®

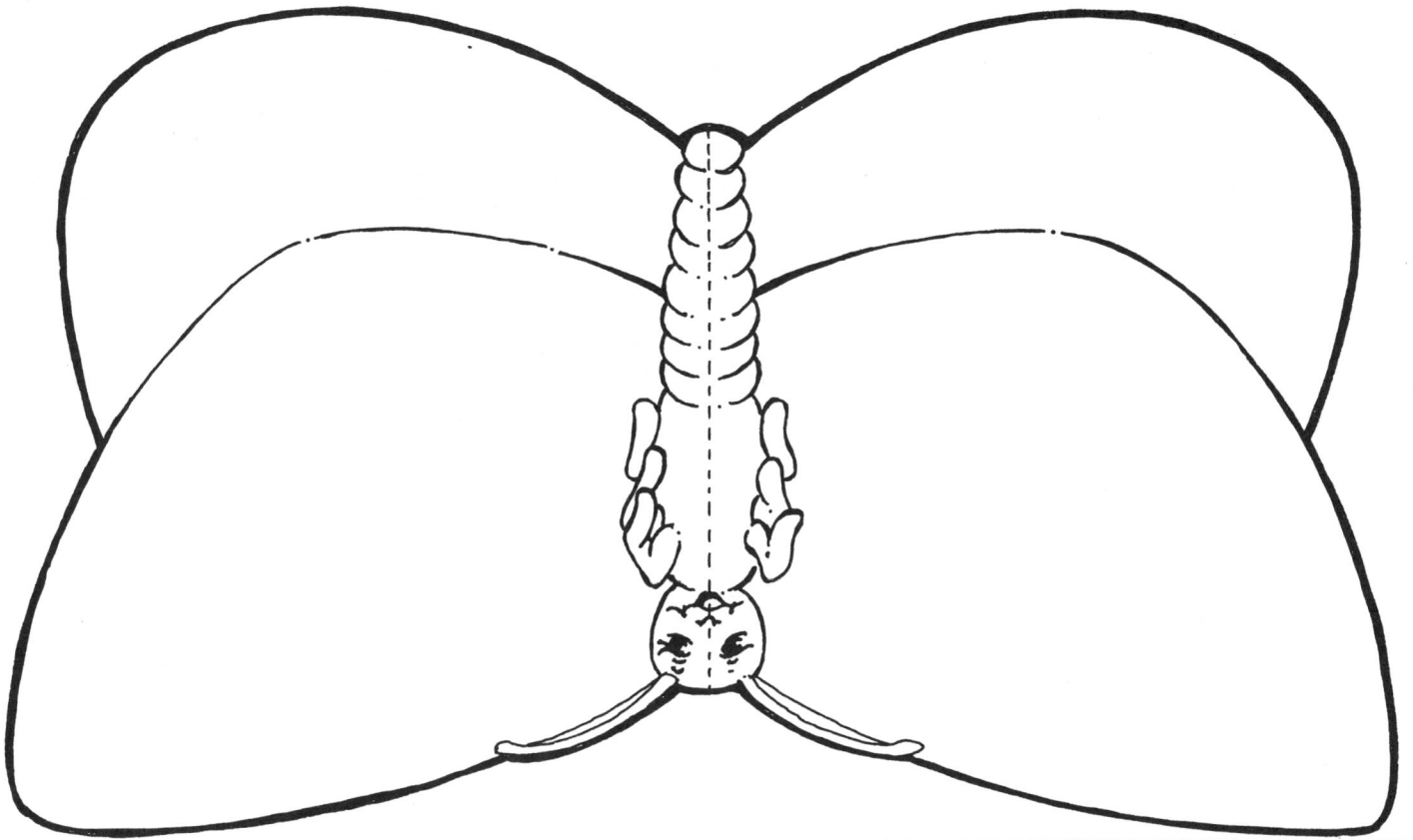
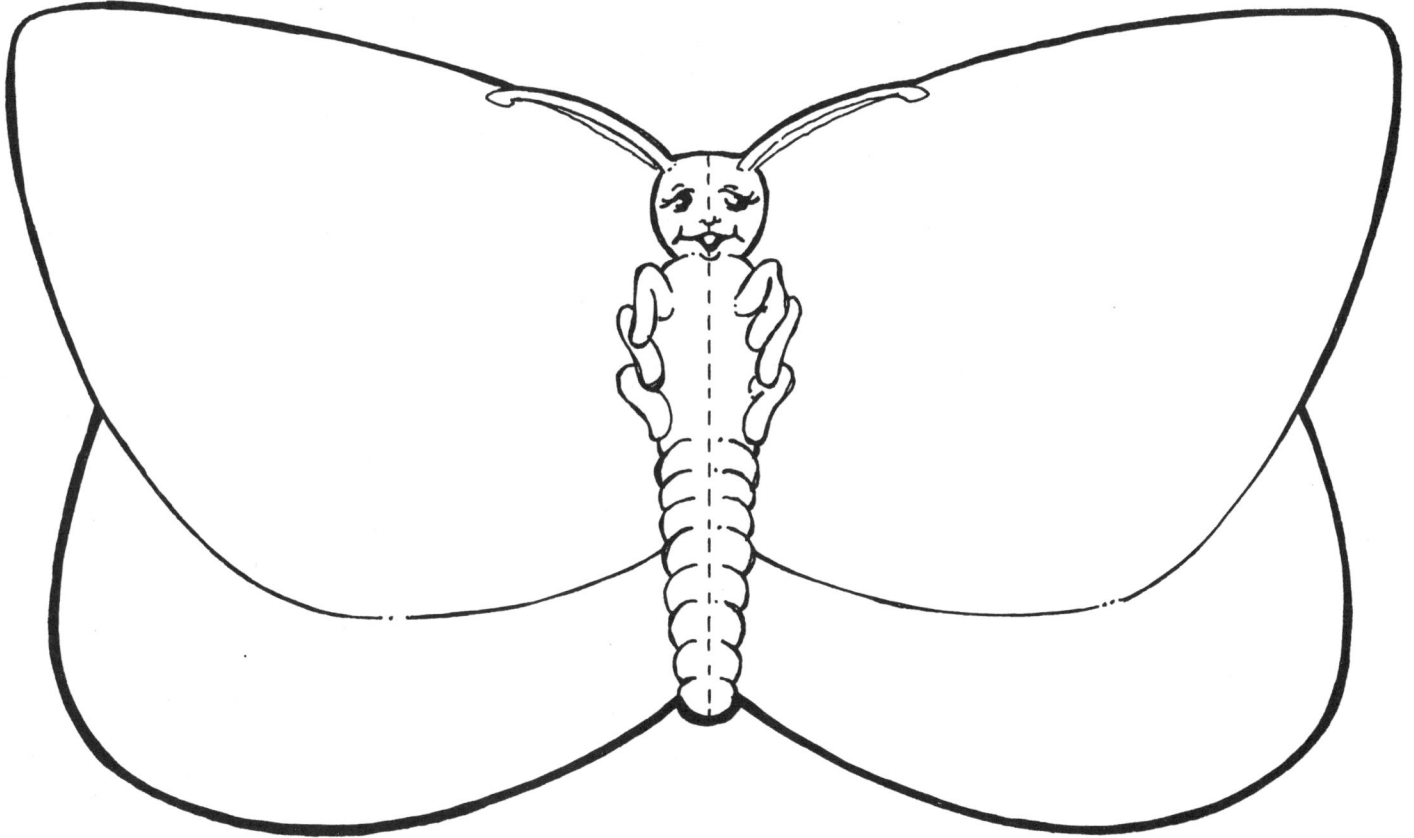

Reproducible 11B

141

On the Road

Enter the ZONE

Bible Verse
Sing for joy to the LORD.
Psalm 98:4, *Good News Bible*

Bible Story
Luke 24:13-35

On the Road to Emmaus occurred one of the most beloved events of the New Testament.

When Jesus died on the cross, the hopes of many of his followers died with him. Of those who heard the women's account of the empty tomb and the meeting with an angel of the Lord, some were more puzzled than convinced.

The two men on the road to Emmaus had yet to figure out exactly what it all meant. This was Easter Day, and though the rumors of crucifixion and even of resurrection were spreading, they had not had time to assimilate it all.

The men did not know that this man accompanying them on their journey was their risen Lord, even when he taught them the meaning of Scriptures. The implication is that it takes an openness to recognize the risen Christ.

Jesus told the men that they were "foolish" and "slow of heart to believe" (Luke 24:25). After admonishing them for their foolishness, he broke bread with them. It was at this point that recognition came. Once they recognized Jesus as the risen Lord, they knew that the signs had been there all along.

It is often the same with us. We are so busy looking for the meaning and purpose of our lives that we miss it until we allow ourselves to become open to it. We have to arrive at Emmaus before we understand that God has been on the journey with us all along.

For young children, emphasize the joy the friends felt when they recognized Jesus. Jesus' friends were excited and ran to share their joy with others.

We celebrate with joy because we know Jesus is alive!

Scope the Zone

ZONE	TIME	SUPPLIES	◎ ZILLIES®
Zoom Into the Zone			
Road Work	15 minutes	Reproducibles 12A and 12B, scissors, crayons or markers, glue; chalk; sand, shallow containers, cotton swabs, shallow tray or box lid	sandpaper
BibleZone®			
Going to Emmaus	5 minutes	none	none
On the Road	10 minutes	road pictures and story figures (Reproducibles 12A and 12B) (optional: large envelopes or resealable plastic bags)	none
Bible Verse Buzz	5 minutes	Bible, BZ Bee	none
Sing!	5 minutes	cassette player	Cassette
LifeZone			
Walk the Walk	10 minutes	Reproducible 12B, scissors	none
Hello, Friend	10 minutes	sheet or towel	none
Where Is Happy?	5 minutes	none	smile face finger puppets
Sign 'n Pray	5 minutes	none	none

◎ Zillies® are found in the **BibleZone® FUNspirational® Kit.**

Choose one or more activities to catch your children's interest.

Supplies:
Reproducibles 12A and 12B, scissors, crayons or markers, glue; chalk; sand, shallow containers, cotton swabs, shallow tray or box lid

Zillies®:
sandpaper

Road Work

(P) hotocopy the road picture **(Reproducible 12A)** and the story figures **(Reproducible 12B)** for each child and for yourself. Cut apart the story figures. Set aside the stop sign to use later in the lesson. Give each child the road picture.

Say: Today our Bible story is about two men who were walking down the road to a town called Emmaus.

Let the children decorate their road pictures with chalk.

Or have the children decorate their road pictures with sand. Have the children color the pictures with crayons. Pour glue into shallow containers and provide cotton swabs. Let the children use cotton swabs to wipe glue onto the road in their pictures. Place each picture in a shallow tray or box lid. Show the children how to sprinkle dry sand over their pictures. Shake off the excess sand into a trash container.

Or have the children decorate their road pictures with **sandpaper**. Have the children color the pictures with crayons. Cut sandpaper into small pieces. Let the children glue the pieces onto their pictures.

Give each child the story figure of Jesus and the story figure of the two friends. Let the children decorate the figures with crayons or markers.

Say: The two men were friends of Jesus. They were sad because they did not know Jesus was alive. As they were walking to Emmaus, a third man began to walk with them. The third man was Jesus! The friends were no longer sad. They were happy and full of joy because they knew Jesus was alive.

ZONE IN | **We celebrate with joy because we know Jesus is alive!**

Help the children fold the story figures along the dotted lines to make the figures stand. Write the children's names on their road pictures and their figures. Have the children place their roads and story figures in your story area. Let glue the dry.

Bible ZONE

Choose one or more activities to immerse your children in the Bible story.

Going to Emmaus

Supplies:
none

Zillies®:
none

Have the children move to an open area of the room.

Say: Jesus died and was buried in a tomb. Two men were walking to a town called Emmaus after Jesus died. They were sad. Show me how you look when you are sad. *(Let the children make sad faces.)* **But something happened on the road to Emmaus. The men saw Jesus! The two men were surprised. Show me how you look when you're surprised.** *(Encourage the children to look surprised.)* **Jesus talked to the men. Jesus was alive! The two men were happy. Show me how you look when you are happy.** *(Encourage the children to look happy.)*

Sing the song printed below to the tune of "This Is the Way" and do the motions with the children.

> This is the way the two men walked,
> *(Walk in place.)*
> Two men walked, two men walked.
> This is the way the two men walked,
> Going to Emmaus.
>
> This is the way the two men looked,
> *(Look surprised.)*
> Two men looked, two men looked.
> This is the way the two men looked
> When they knew it was Jesus.
>
> This is the way the two men ran,
> *(Run in place.)*
> Two men ran, two men ran.
> This is the way the two men ran
> To tell the good news.

Words: Linda Ray Miller and Daphna Flegal
© 1997 Abingdon Press.

We celebrate with joy because we know Jesus is alive!

On the Road

by Daphna Flegal

Encourage the children to bring their road pictures and story figures (**Reproducibles 12A and 12B**) and to sit down around a table or on the floor. Have the children place their road pictures in front of them. Instruct the children to set the story figures of the two men at the beginning of the road. Keep the story figure of Jesus to the side. Sit with the children and use the road and story figures you prepared for yourself.

Say: Let's move our story figures down the road as I tell the story.

(Place the two men story figures at the beginning of the road.)

Two men were walking down a road to a town called Emmaus. They were friends of Jesus. They were very sad. They thought their friend Jesus was dead.

(Move the figures down the road.)

As they were walking, they talked about Jesus. Then a stranger started walking with them. They did not know who the stranger was.

(Add the Jesus figure.)

"What are you talking about as you walk along?" asked the stranger.

"Don't you know what has happened?" answered one of the men. "Our friend Jesus is dead. He was buried in a garden tomb."

The stranger listened to the two men. Then he started telling them about God, just like their friend Jesus used to do.

(Move the three figures down the road.)

Soon the three men came to Emmaus. The two men invited the stranger to stay with them. The three men sat down to eat together.

(Move the three figures to the end of the road.)

The stranger took the bread from the table and broke it apart. He said a thank-you prayer for the bread. Then the two men knew who the stranger was! It was Jesus! Jesus was alive!

(Take the Jesus figure from the road. Move the two men quickly back to the beginning.)

Jesus left, and the two men ran back to tell their friends the good news. Jesus was alive!

Teacher Tip: Place the road pictures and story figures in large envelopes or resealable plastic bags for the children to take home.

Bible Verse Buzz

Choose a child to hold the Bible open to Psalm 98:4.

Say: Today our Bible story is about two men who were walking down the road to a town called Emmaus. They were sad because they did not know Jesus was alive. As they were walking, a third man began to walk with them. The third man was Jesus! The friends were no longer sad. They were full of joy because they knew Jesus was alive.

Say the Bible verse, "Sing for joy to the LORD" (Psalm 98:4, *Good News Bible*), for the children. Have the children say the Bible verse after you.

Turn your back to the children or hide your hands underneath a table or behind the **BibleZone® FUNspirational® Kit** lid as you place the **BZ Bee puppet** (see page 174) on your hand. Turn around or bring the puppet out where the children can see it.

Pretend to make the puppet talk. Change your voice for the puppet:

Bzzz. Bzzz. Bzzz. Hi, everybody! I'm BZ Bee. *Bzzz. Bzzz. Bzzz.* I like to taste fingers. Do you have fingers? Yum, yum, yum. Let me taste.

Go to each child. Encourage, but do not force, each child to hold up his or her fingers. Have BZ pretend to taste each child's fingers. Have BZ say things like:

Mmmm. Mmmm. You taste like honey. *Bzzz. Bzzz.* You taste like strawberries. *Yumm. Yumm.* You taste like blueberries.

After BZ has tasted each child's fingers, say:

Bzzz. Bzzz. Bzzz. I like to taste your fingers. They're yummy. *(Rub BZ's stomach.)*

Bzzz. Bzzz. Bzzz. I like something else even more than fingers.

I like the Bible. *Bzzz. Bzzz. Bzzz.* You heard a Bible story today. Who were walking down the road to Emmaus? *(two men, friends of Jesus)* Who did the men see that surprised them? *(Jesus)*

Bzzz. Bzzz. Bzzz. When the two men saw that Jesus was alive, the men were happy and filled with joy.

We celebrate with joy because we know Jesus is alive!

Bzzz. Bzzz. Bzzz. Let's all say the Bible verse together.

"Sing for joy to the LORD" (Psalm 98:4, *Good News Bible*).

Have the children repeat the Bible verse with BZ Bee.

Have BZ Bee say goodbye to the children.

Bible Zone®

Choose one or more activities to immerse your children in the Bible story.

Supplies:
cassette player

Zillies®:
Cassette

Sing!

Have the children move to an open area of the room.

Say: When the two men knew that Jesus was alive, they were happy and filled with joy.

> **Zone In®** We celebrate with joy because we know Jesus is alive!

Play the song "Ha-Le-La-Le-La-Le-Lu-Jah" from the **Cassette**. Let the children dance as the music plays.

Ha-Le-La-Le-La-Le-Lu-Jah

Hal-le-la-le-la-le-lu-jah,
Hal-le-lu-jah to the Lord,
Hal-le-la-le-la-le-lu-jah,
Praise His name forevermore.
Hal-le-la-le-la-le-lu-jah,
Lift your voice, rejoice and sing
Hal-le-la-le-la-le-lu-jah,
to the King of Kings!

He is the Holy One,
Jesus, God's only Son,
crowning glory of all creation,
clap your hands in celebration!

Hal-le-la-le-la-le-lu-jah,
Hal-le-lu-jah to the Lord,
Hal-le-la-le-la-le-lu-jah,
Praise His name forevermore.
Hal-le-la-le-la-le-lu-jah,
Lift your voice, rejoice and sing
Hal-le-la-le-la-le-lu-jah,
to the King of Kings!

He is the Holy One,
Jesus, God's only Son,
crowning glory of all creation,
clap your hands in celebration!

Hal-le-la-le-la-le-lu-jah,
Hal-le-lu-jah to the Lord,
Hal-le-la-le-la-le-lu-jah,
Praise His name forevermore.
Hal-le-la-le-la-le-lu-jah,
Lift your voice, rejoice and sing
Hal-le-la-le-la-le-lu-jah,
to the King of Kings!

Hal-le-la-le-la-le-lu-jah,
to the King of Kings!

Writers: Janet McMahan-Wilson and Ted Wilson

Walk the Walk

Supplies:
Reproducible 12B, scissors

Zillies®:
none

(P)hotocopy and cut apart the stop sign **(Reproducible 12B).** Have the children move to one side of the room.

Say: Today our Bible story is about two men who were walking down the road to a town called Emmaus. They were sad because they did not know Jesus was alive. As they were walking, a third man began to walk with them. The third man was Jesus! The friends were no longer sad. They were full of joy because they knew Jesus was alive.

Have each child choose a friend to be her or his partner. Have the children stand with their friends. If you have an uneven number of children, let one group have three friends. Have the children stand on one side of the room. You hold the stop sign and stand on the other side of the room.

Say: Let's pretend we are the two friends of Jesus walking down the road. Walk with your friends towards me. When you see me hold up the stop sign, stop wherever you are and freeze. When I say the Bible verse, you can start walking again.

Have the children start walking towards you. After a few seconds, hold up the stop sign and have the children freeze in place. Say the Bible verse, "Sing for joy to the LORD" (Psalm 98:4, *Good News Bible*), and have the children start walking again. Stop the game when all the children reach you.

Repeat the game as the children show interest and vary how the children walk across the room (*walk like you are sad, walk like you are happy, walk like it is a very hot day, walk like it is a very cold day, walk backwards, and so forth*).

Hello, Friend

Supplies:
sheet or towel

Zillies®:
none

(S)ay: **At first the two men walking to Emmaus did not know that the stranger walking with them was their friend Jesus. Let's play a game to see if we know our friends.**

Have the children sit down in a circle. Choose a child to be the guesser and to sit in the center of the circle. Drape a sheet or towel over the guesser's head. Choose another child in the circle to say, "Hello, friend, it's me." Have the guesser try to guess who is speaking. Let the two children switch places. Continue the game until each child has had an opportunity to be the guesser.

Life Zone ®

Choose one or more activities to bring the Bible to life.

Where Is Happy?

Have the children sit in a circle. Give each child two **smile face finger puppets.** Help each child put a finger puppet on each thumb. Lead the children in the fingerplay song below to the tune of "Are You Sleeping?"

Where is Happy?
(Put finger puppets behind your back.)
Where is Happy?
(Put finger puppets behind your back.)
Here I am!
(Bring one finger puppet to the front.)
Here I am!
(Bring second finger puppet to the front.)

Listen to God's Word now.
(Bend one finger puppet.)
Listen to God's Word now.
(Bend second finger puppet.)
Sing for joy
(Hold one finger puppet to ear.)
To the LORD!
(Hold second finger puppet to other ear.)

Sign 'n Pray

Have the children sit in a circle on the floor. Teach the children the Bible verse in American Sign Language. Go around the circle and name each child.

Say: *(Child's name),* **sing for joy to the LORD.**

© 1998 Abingdon Press

Have the child sign the verse with you.

Pray: Thank you, God, for the good news that Jesus is alive. Amen.

Photocopy the **HomeZone®** newsletter to send home to parents.

150

Bible Verse
Sing for joy to the LORD.
Psalm 98:4, Good News Bible

Bible Story
Luke 24:13-35

On the Road

Today your child heard the Bible story of the two men who were walking on the road to Emmaus. They were sad because they did not know Jesus was alive. As they were walking, a third man began to walk with them. They did not recognize the man, but they talked to him and told him about the death of their friend Jesus. When the men arrived in Emmaus, they invited the stranger to stay and to eat with them. When the stranger broke the bread, they realized he was Jesus! The two men were no longer sad. They were full of joy because they knew that Jesus was alive.

Where Is Happy?

Enjoy the fingerplay printed below with your child. Remind your child that we are happy to know that Jesus is alive.

Where is Happy?
(Put hands behind your back.)
Where is Happy?
(Put hands behind your back.)
Here I am!
(Hold up one thumb; bring to the front.)
Here I am!
(Hold up other thumb; bring to the front.)

Listen to God's Word now.
(Bend one thumb.)
Listen to God's Word now.
(Bend second thumb.)
Sing for joy
(Hold one thumb to ear.)
To the LORD!
(Hold second thumb to other ear.)

ZONE IN

We celebrate with joy because we know Jesus is alive!

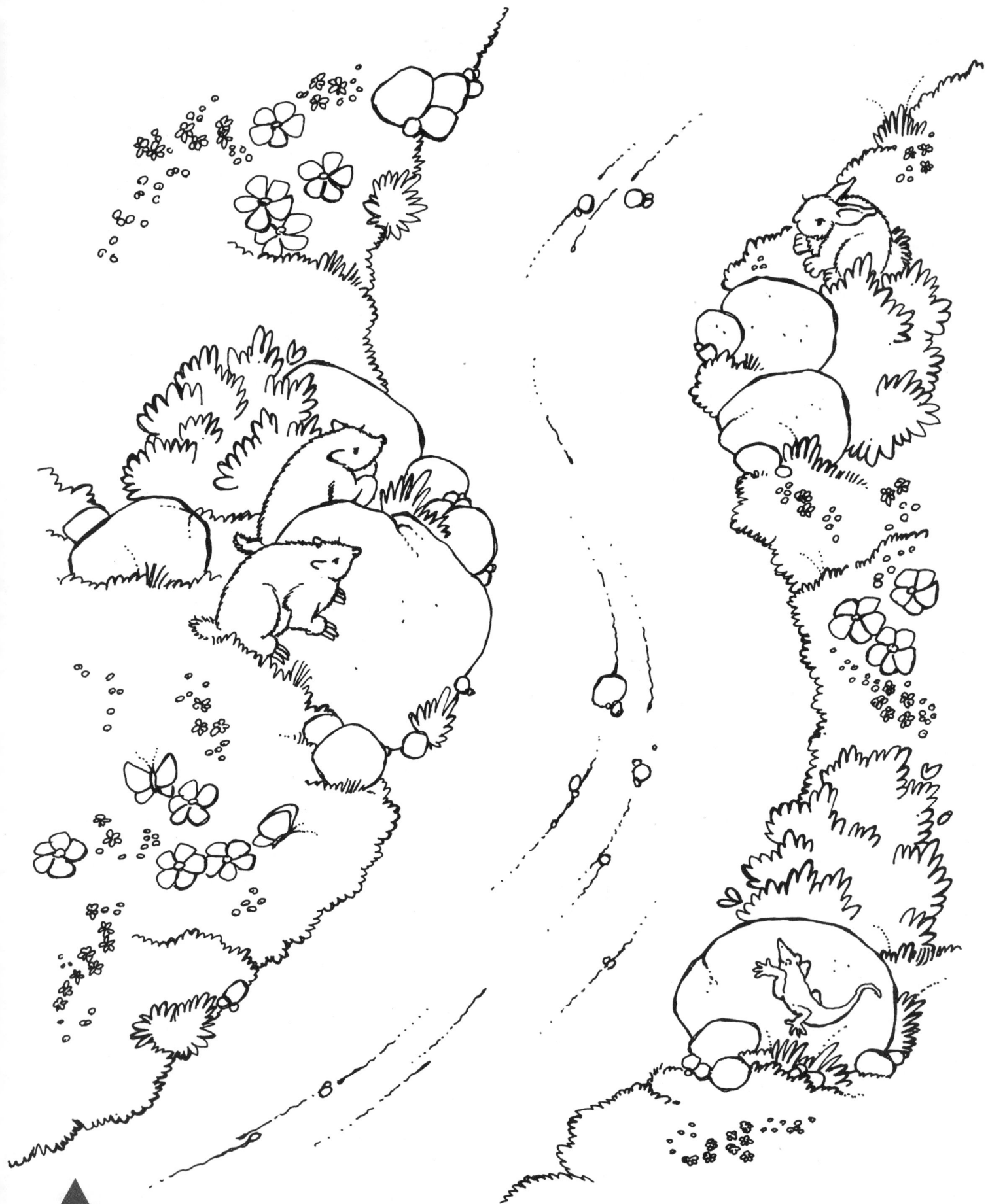

Reproducible 12A

Permission granted to photocopy for local church use. © 1999 Abingdon Press.

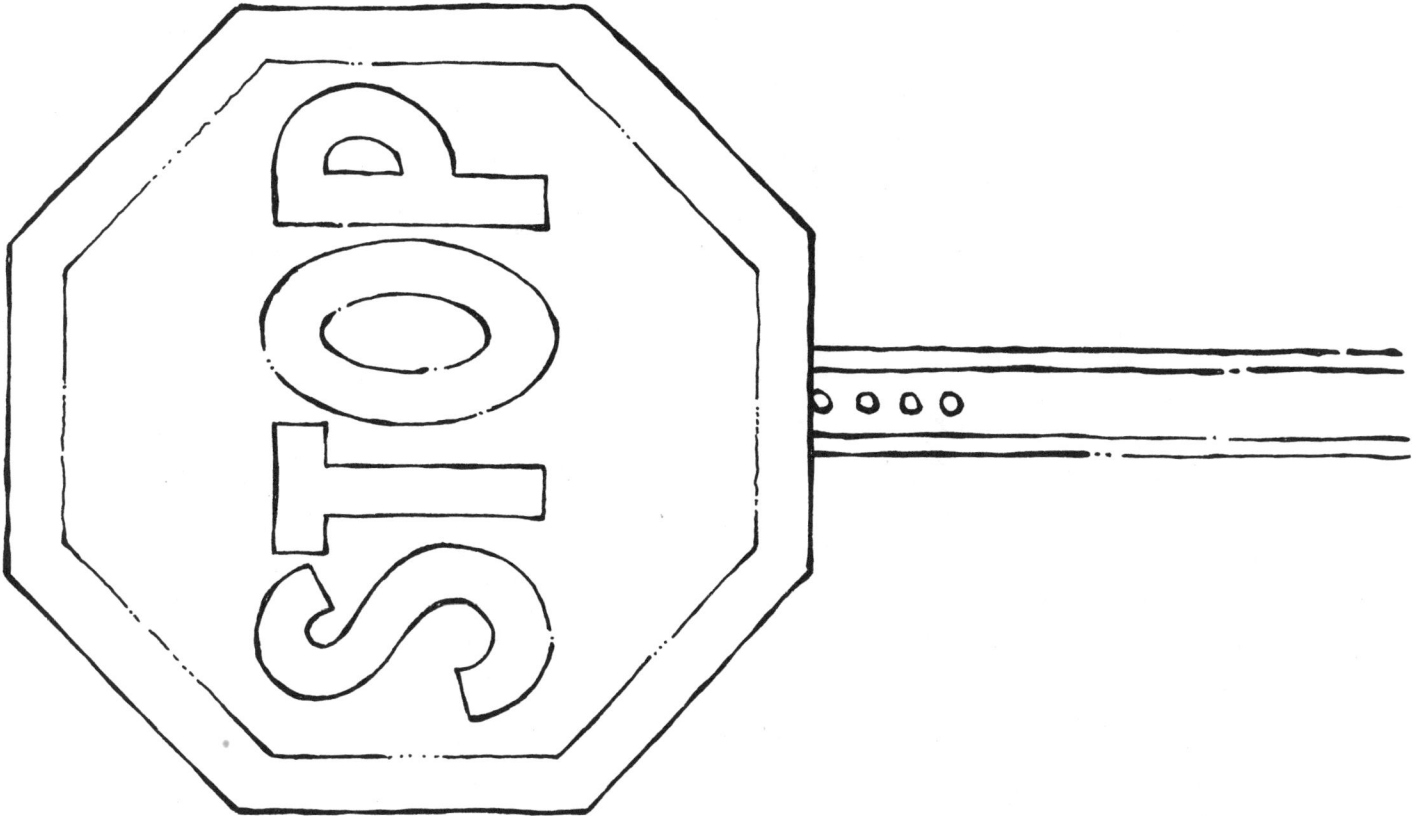

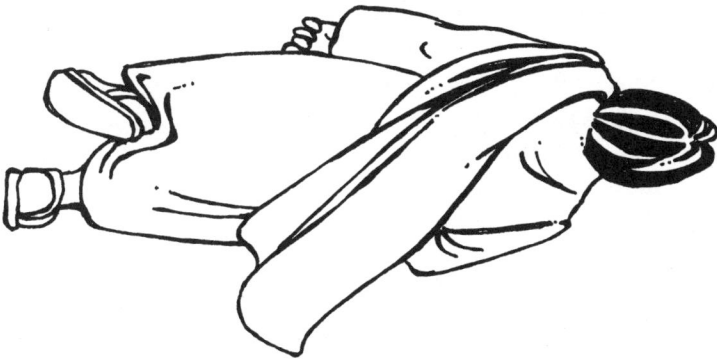
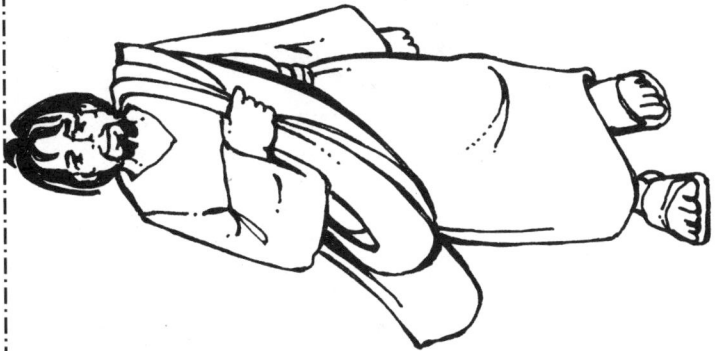

Reproducible 12B

With Us Always

Enter the **ZONE**

Bible Verse
And remember, I am with you always.
Matthew 28:20

Bible Story
Matthew 28:16-20; Mark 16:14-18;
Luke 24:36-49; John 20:19-23

When something is recorded in all four Gospels, we can be sure that it has great importance.

The risen Christ's appearance to the disciples and his commissioning them to go into all the world is at the center of who and what we are. We have the good news of our new relationship with God.

Telling the world about all they knew and had learned was Jesus' commission for the disciples. In Matthew 28:19 we read the command to baptize "in the name of the Father and of the Son and of the Holy Spirit."

The main tasks of the disciples were to baptize and to teach. To this small group of unlikely people was given the task of sharing with the world the love and the great sacrifice of God.

The world for these men was a hard and unforgiving place, and the task would not be an easy one. They were ill-equipped in their lack of formal education and even natural abilities. But they were given the one gift that made it possible for them to carry out their task—the presence of Jesus Christ, their Lord. This gift was given to them through the Holy Spirit. Jesus said, "Remember, I am with you always" (Matthew 28:20). That promise was kept.

The promise is for us also. If we will accept the challenge of living so that all will know the great love of God, we will not be alone, ever! All we have to do is open our hearts. The Holy Spirit is with us always.

Scope the ZONE

ZONE	TIME	SUPPLIES	⊚ ZILLIES®
Zoom Into the Zone			
Time Out	10 minutes	Reproducible 13A, scissors, crayons or markers, tape	none
Memory Work	10 minutes	tray or table	camel beanbag, celestial ball, star glitter wand, smile face finger puppet
BibleZone®			
It's Time	5 minutes	none	none
Sign 'n Say	5 minutes	none	none
Go to Galilee	10 minutes	none	none
Bible Verse Buzz	5 minutes	Bible, BZ Bee	none
Sing!	5 minutes	cassette player	Cassette
LifeZone			
Shake and Think	10 minutes	paper watches (Reproducible 13A), Reproducible 13B, Bible, scissors, paper bag	none
Happy Stamps	10 minutes	newspaper, paint smocks, paper towels, shallow trays, tempera paint, construction paper, soap and water, marker	smile face finger puppets
Beanbag Prayers	5 minutes	none	smile face beanbag key chain

⊚ Zillies® are found in the **BibleZone® FUNspirational® Kit.**

Choose one or more activities to catch your children's interest.

Supplies:
Reproducible 13A, scissors, crayons or markers, tape

Zillies®:
none

Time Out

(P)hotocopy and cut apart the watch strips **(Reproducible 13A)**. You will need one strip for each child and one for yourself. Let the children decorate the strips with crayons or markers. Tape each child's strip around her or his wrist. Encourage the children to wear the strips on their wrists as pretend watches.

Say: **Today our Bible story is about Jesus and his helpers. Jesus told his helpers to remember something special. He told them that he would always be with them.**

Jesus is with us all the time.

Supplies:
tray or table

Zillies®:
camel beanbag, celestial ball, star glitter wand, smile face finger puppet

Memory Work

(P)lace several Zillies® such as the **camel beanbag**, the **celestial ball**, the **star glitter wand**, and a **smile face finger puppet** on a tray or on the table.

Show the children the items and name each item for the children. Have the children cover their eyes with their hands or turn their backs. Take away one of the items and hide it behind your back or under the table. Have the children uncover their eyes or turn around. Encourage the children to remember which item is missing. After the children guess, put the item back with the others.

Play the game several times, removing different items. You may make the game more difficult by removing two or three items at a time.

Say: **You are good at remembering! Today our Bible story is about Jesus and his helpers. Jesus told his helpers to remember something special. He told them that he would always be with them.**

Jesus is with us all the time.

Bible ZONE®

Choose one or more activities to immerse your children in the Bible story.

It's Time

(**L**)ead your children to your story area with the following activity.

It's time to hear a story,
(Tap wrist as if pointing to a watch.)
So come with me right now.
(Motion "come here.")
Just follow me as I go.
(March in place.)
I will show you how.
(Point to self; point to others.)

Let's hop! *(Hop around the room.)*
Let's tiptoe! *(Tiptoe around the room.)*
Let's march! *(March to your story area.)*

It's time to hear a story,
(Tap wrist as if pointing to a watch.)
So come with me right now.
(Motion "come here.")
Just follow me as I go.
(March in place.)
I will show you how.
(Point to self; point to others.)

Let's sit!
(Sit down in your story area.)

Supplies:
none

Zillies®:
none

Sign 'n Say

(**T**)each the children the Bible verse, "And remember, I am with you always" (Matthew 28:20), in American Sign Language.

Supplies:
none

Zillies®:
none

I—Hold up little finger, with the other fingers curled down. Place at chest. With—Hold both hands in fists, with thumbs on the outside. Place the fists together, palms touching. You—Point out with your index finger. Always—Hold out your index finger with your palm facing up. Draw a circle in front of your body.

Go to Galilee

by Daphna Flegal

Invite the children to stand in a circle. Tell the children the story. Have the children march in place each time you begin the rhyme. Have the children shout the name "Jesus!" at the end of the rhyme.

Jesus' helpers were happy. They knew Jesus was alive. They were going to a mountain in Galilee to meet Jesus.

(March in place.)
Go, go, go,
Let's go to Galilee.
Go, go, go,
Who do you think we'll see?

(Have the children shout.)
Jesus!

Jesus' helpers climbed up the mountain.

(March in place.)
Go, go, go,
Let's go to Galilee.
Go, go, go,
Who do you think we'll see?

(Have the children shout.)
Jesus!

They were very happy when they saw Jesus.

"Go and tell all the people about me," said Jesus. "Help all the people become my followers."

(March in place.)
Go, go, go,
Let's go to Galilee.
Go, go, go,
Who do you think we'll see?

(Have the children shout.)
Jesus!

Jesus looked at each one of his helpers. "Remember," said Jesus. "I am with you always."

(March in place.)
Go, go, go,
Let's go to Galilee.
Go, go, go,
Who do you think we'll see?

(Have the children shout.)
Jesus!

Jesus' helpers did what Jesus told them to do. They went to many, many places and told many, many people about Jesus.

Jesus' helpers remembered what Jesus said. They remembered that Jesus was with them all the time.

(March in place.)
Go, go, go,
Let's go to Galilee.
Go, go, go,
Who do you think we'll see?

(Have the children shout.)
Jesus!

Bible Verse Buzz

Choose a child to hold the Bible open to Matthew 28:20.

Say: Today our Bible story is about Jesus and his helpers. Jesus told his helpers to remember something special. He told them that he would always be with them.

Say the Bible verse, "And remember, I am with you always" (Matthew 28:20), for the children. Have the children say the Bible verse after you.

Turn your back to the children or hide your hands underneath a table or behind the **BibleZone® FUNspirational® Kit** lid as you place the **BZ Bee puppet** (see page 174) on your hand. Turn around or bring the puppet out where the children can see it.

Pretend to make the puppet talk. Change your voice for the puppet:

Bzzz. Bzzz. Bzzz. Hi, everybody! I'm BZ Bee. *Bzzz. Bzzz. Bzzz.* I like to taste fingers. Do you have fingers? Yum, yum, yum. Let me taste.

Go to each child. Encourage, but do not force, each child to hold up his or her fingers. Have BZ pretend to taste each child's fingers. Have BZ say things like:

Mmmm. Mmmm. You taste like honey.
Bzzz. Bzzz. You taste like strawberries.
Yumm. Yumm. You taste like blueberries.

After BZ has tasted each child's fingers, say:

Bzzz. Bzzz. Bzzz. I like to taste your fingers. They're yummy. *(Rub BZ's stomach.)*

Bzzz. Bzzz. Bzzz. I like something else even more than fingers.

I like the Bible. *Bzzz. Bzzz. Bzzz.* You heard a Bible story today. Who was the story about? *(Jesus)* What did Jesus tell his helpers? *(that he would always be with them)*

Bzzz. Bzzz. Bzzz. When Jesus told his helpers that he would always be with them, they were happy.

> **Jesus is with us all the time.**

Bzzz. Bzzz. Bzzz. Let's all say the Bible verse together.

"And remember, I am with you always" (Matthew 28:20).

Have the children repeat the Bible verse with BZ Bee.

Have BZ Bee say goodbye to the children.

Bible Zone

Supplies:
cassette player

Zillies®:
Cassette

Sing!

Say: Today our Bible story is about Jesus and his helpers. Jesus told his helpers to remember something special. He told them that he would always be with them. Jesus also wanted his friends to go to all people everywhere and to tell them about Jesus.

Sing together the song "Give and Go" from the **Cassette.** Follow the directions printed in italics for movement.

Give and Go

Give and go,
(Walk around the circle.)
give and go,
so that all the world may know;
give and go,
(Walk around the circle the other way.)
give and go,
Jesus loves them so.
(Stop; put hands over heart.)

Ev'ry nation,
(Sweep arms up over head and out.)
Ev'ry land,
(Turn around.)
they must hear and understand.
(Cup hands around ears.)
Give and go,
(Walk around the circle the other way.)
give and go,
Jesus loves them so.
(Stop; put hands over heart.)

Give and go,
(Walk around the circle.)
give and go,
so that all the world may know;
give and go,
(Walk around the circle the other way.)
give and go,
Jesus loves them so.
(Stop; put hands over heart.)

Ev'ry nation,
(Sweep arms up over head and out.)
Ev'ry land,
(Turn around.)
they must hear and understand.
(Cup hands around ears.)
Give and go,
(Walk around the circle the other way.)
give and go,
Jesus loves them so.
(Stop; put hands over heart.)

Writer: Ruth Schram

From the Brentwood-Benson Music Publishing, Inc. recording, *Mother Goose Gospel, Vol. 1.*

Shake and Think

(P) hotocopy and cut apart the picture cards **(Reproducible 13B)**. You will need at least one picture for each child. Place the cards in a paper bag. Have the children sit in a circle on the floor. Encourage the children to wear their paper watches **(Reproducible 13A)** for this activity. Put a paper watch on your own wrist.

Say: Today our Bible story is about Jesus and his helpers. Jesus told his helpers to remember something special. He told them that he would always be with them. Let's think about the times when Jesus is with us.

Give the child next to you the bag. Have the child shake the bag to mix up the cards. Let the child open the bag, reach in, and pull out one card. Have the child show the children the picture on the card.

Ask: What is the child doing in the picture? *(Let the children respond and name whatever the child is doing in the picture.)* **Is Jesus with us when we (name whatever the child is doing in the picture)?**

Hold up the arm with the paper watch and **say: Yes! Jesus is with us all the time!** *(Have the children repeat.)*

Have the child place the picture on the floor in front of him or her. Continue passing the bag around the circle and let each child have a turn shaking the bag and pulling out a picture. Ask the questions and say the *yes* affirmation each time.

When every child has had a turn, have all the children pick up the picture cards they placed on the floor. Hold an open Bible. Go to each child in the circle and have the child place the picture on the open Bible. Help the child repeat the Bible verse, "And remember, I am with you always" (Matthew 28:20). Place the open Bible with the picture cards in your worship area.

ZONE IN

Jesus is with us all the time.

Supplies:
paper watches (Reproducible 13A), Reproducible 13B, Bible, scissors, paper bag

Zillies®:

Supplies:
newspaper, paint smocks, paper towels, shallow trays, tempera paint, construction paper, soap and water, marker

Zillies®:
smile face finger puppets

Happy Stamps

Cover the table with newspapers and have the children wear paint smocks. Fold paper towels and place them in shallow trays. Pour tempera paint onto the paper towels to make a paint pad. If possible, prepare two or more colors of paint pads.

Say: **Today our Bible story is about Jesus and his helpers. Jesus told his helpers to remember something special. He told them that he would always be with them. When Jesus' helpers saw Jesus and heard what Jesus told them, they were very happy. Let's make happy pictures to help us remember that Jesus is with us all the time.**

If you wish, print the Bible verse, "And remember, I am with you always" (Matthew 28:20), across each child's paper before class. Give each child a piece of construction paper (with or without the Bible verse).

Give each child a **smile face finger puppet** to make circles on their papers. Show the children how to hold the finger puppets by their heads and arms and press the bottoms of the puppets onto the paint pad and then onto their papers. Encourage the children to use different colors and to make several prints with the finger puppets. Set the pictures flat to dry. When you are finished with this activity, wash the finger puppets with soap and water so they can be used again.

Supplies:
none

Zillies®:
smile face beanbag key chain

Beanbag Prayers

Have the children sit in a circle on the floor. Show the children the **smile face beanbag key chain.**

Say: **Jesus promised to be with his friends all the time. We are friends of Jesus. We know that Jesus is with us all the time.**

Walk around the inside of the circle. Hold the beanbag over each child.

Say: **I am happy that Jesus is with** (child's name). **Thank you, God, for** (child's name). **Amen.**

Continue around the circle until you have prayed for every child.

Photocopy the **HomeZone**® newsletter to send home to parents.

Bible Verse
And remember, I am with you always.
Matthew 28:20

Bible Story
Matthew 28:16-20; Mark 16:14-18; Luke 24:36-49; John 20:19-23

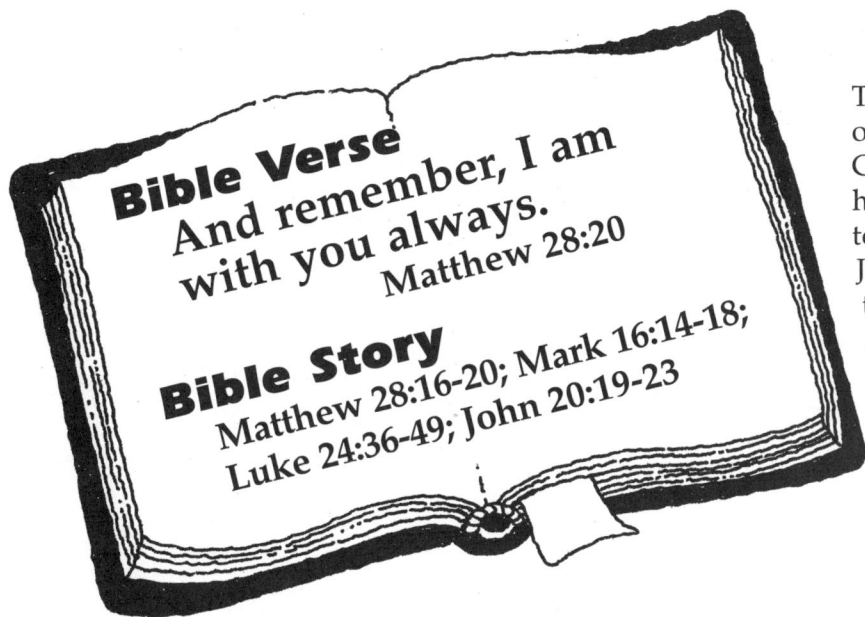

With Us Always

Today your child heard the Bible story of when the disciples met the risen Christ in Galilee. When Jesus met with his disciples, he told them to go and tell all people everywhere about him. Jesus also told his friends to remember that he would be with them always. As followers of Jesus, we can claim that promise for ourselves. Jesus is with us all the time.

Sign 'n Say

Help your child learn the Bible verse, "And remember, I am with you always" (Matthew 28:20), in American Sign Language.

I—Hold up little finger, with the other fingers curled down. Place at chest.
With—Hold both hands in fists, with thumbs on the outside. Place the fists together, palms touching.
You—Point out with your index finger.
Always—Hold out your index finger with your palm facing up. Draw a circle in front of your body.

| I | With |
| You | Always |

Jesus is with us all the time.

Jesus is with us all the time.

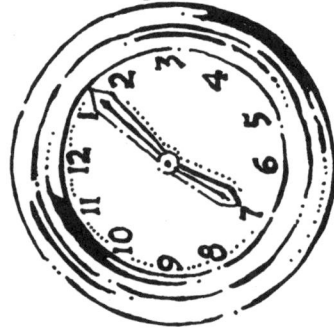

Jesus is with us all the time.

Jesus is with us all the time.

Jesus is with us all the time.

Jesus is with us all the time

Jesus is with us all the time

Jesus is with us all the time

Jesus is with us all the time

Reproducible 13A

BIBLEZONE®

Sleeping

Eating

Running

Building

Dancing

Hopping

Happy

Sad

Reproducible 13B

Birthday Zone

Birthday Cheer

Use the suggestions in this Birthday Zone to celebrate birthdays. Have the children make a circle around the birthday child. Let the children walk in a circle around the child as you say:

Hip, hip, hooray,
It's *(child's name)*'s special day.
Let's gather near
And give a cheer.
Hip, hip, hooray!

Have the children stop walking, jump up, and cheer for the child.

Birthday Buzz

Show the children the **BZ Bee puppet**. Pretend to fly the puppet around the room as you **say:**

BZ Bee is buzzing
All around the room.
He's buzzing to the birthday girl *(boy)*.
Zoom, zoom, zoom.

Stop at the birthday child and have BZ Bee give the child a hug.

Birthday Jingle

Sing this song to the tune of "This Is the Way" to celebrate a child's birthday.

This is the way we light the candles,
Light the candles, light the candles.
This is the way we light the candles
On our birthday cake.

1, 2, 3, 4
(Count the number of candles for the child's age. Hold up a finger for each candle. Pretend to light the tip of each finger.)

Our friend *(child's name)* is four *(use correct age)* today,
Four today, four today.
Our friend *(child's name)* is four today,
Happy birthday, *(child's name)*.

Follow me to a Happy Birthday!

Sing for Joy

(U)se the songs in this SongZone when you need a few minutes to get the wiggles out. All the songs are to familiar tunes.

Jesus Is Alive

(S)ing this song to the tune of "The Farmer in the Dell."

Oh Jesus is alive.
Oh Jesus is alive.
Oh listen to the news we tell.
Oh Jesus is alive.

Twinkle, Twinkle, Shining Star

(S)ing this song to the tune of "Twinkle, Twinkle, Little Star."

Twinkle, twinkle, shining star,
Guiding wise men from afar,
To a home so far away,
Where little Jesus played all day.
Twinkle, twinkle, shining star,
Guiding wise men from afar.

Words: Sue Downing
© 1990 Graded Press

Song Zone

Let the children listen to the song "The Bible Zone" from the **Cassette** as they enter the room or while working on lesson activities.

The Bible Zone

Where else can we find a lesson learned on every page?
Stories that have lived to teach us all from age to age.
From the flood to parting waters, burning bushes,
    prophets, scholars,
God's Word takes us anywhere.

In the Bible zone where God's Word comes to life.
In the Bible zone our path is always bright.
A book for all creation to every boy and girl.
In the Bible zone is God's treasure for the world.

In the Bible zone where God's Word comes to life.
In the Bible zone our path is always bright.
A book for all creation to every boy and girl.
In the Bible zone is God's treasure for the world.

Learning of forgiveness or when learning how to pray,
God's Word gives examples of the things we face each day.
When we choose to look inside, we see ahead or back in time.
God's Word takes us anywhere.

In the Bible zone where God's Word comes to life.
In the Bible zone our path is always bright.
A book for all creation to every boy and girl.
In the Bible zone is God's treasure for the world.

In the Bible zone where God's Word comes to life.
In the Bible zone our path is always bright.
A book for all creation to every boy and girl.
In the Bible zone is God's treasure for the world.

Words by David Hampton
© 1997 New Spring Publishing, Inc. (ASCAP)
A div. of Brentwood-Benson Music, Inc. All rights reserved. Used by permission.

Sand Painting

Supplies needed: sand, food coloring, container with lid, glue, water, heavy cardboard, shallow containers, cotton swabs, tray or box lid

Make colored sand by mixing 1 pint of sand with 4 to 8 drops of food coloring in a container with a lid. Put the lid on the container and let the children shake the container until all the sand is colored.

Thin glue with water. Pour the glue into shallow containers and provide cotton swabs. Let the children wipe the glue on the heavy cardboard with the cotton swabs. Place the cardboard in a tray or box lid while the glue is still wet. Let the children sprinkle sand over the glue. When the glue has had time to set, shake off the excess sand into a trash container. Repeat with different colors of sand.

Remind the children that when Jesus was a man, he went into the desert,

Scented Stars

*Supplies needed: **sandpaper**, cinnamon sticks, scissors, paper punch, yarn or **ribbon**, tape*

Cut **sandpaper** into star shapes. You can use the star on **Reproducible 2B** as a pattern. Tape a sandpaper star to the table in front of each child. Give each child a cinnamon stick. Show the children how to rub the cinnamon stick across the sandpaper. Use a paper punch to make a hole in the top of each star. Tie a loop of yarn or **ribbon** through each hole to make a hanger. Let the children use the scented stars as tree ornaments.

Remind the children that the wise men followed the star to find Jesus.

170

Tasty Treats

Let the children make and enjoy snacks. Talk about the Bible story as you make and eat the treats. Each recipe is easy for young children to make with a little help from you. And each of these recipes relates to a Bible story in this BibleZone® unit.

Christmas Sandwiches

bread
cheese slices
mayonnaise or mustard
bologna
Christmas cookie cutters

Let the children cut the bread, meat, and cheese with Christmas cookie cutters. Have the children stack the layers together. Add mayonnaise or mustard if desired. Serve the Christmas sandwiches during Lessons 1 or 2.

Blue Gelatin

four small packages or two large packages of blue gelatin
2½ cups boiling water
table knives or dove cookie cutters

Empty gelatin into a large mixing bowl. Pour the boiling water into the bowl and stir until the gelatin is completely dissolved. Pour the gelatin into a 13- by 9-inch pan. Place the pan in the refrigerator until the gelatin is set.

When ready to serve, partially fill a sink with warm water. Dip the bottom of the pan into the warm water for about 15 seconds. Let the children use table knives to cut the gelatin into squares. Or use dove cookie cutters to cut out dove shapes.

Makes about 24 servings. Use with Lesson 4.

Bible ZONE®

Bible ZONE®

Bible ZONE®

Bible ZONE®

Bible ZONE®

Bible ZONE®

Bible ZONE®

Bible ZONE®

All About

_____
(Child's name)

Parent's Name_____

Address_____

_____Telephone Number_____

Child's Birthday_____Age_____

Child's Brothers and Sisters:

Name_____Age_____

Name_____Age_____

Name_____Age_____

Grandparents or other relatives your child sees often and is close to

_____

Nursery school, daycare, or other programs your child attends

_____

Allergies or situations in your child's life that the teacher should know

_____

_____

Parents will be at

_____

173

Bible ZONE 10

Comments From Users

Use the following scale to rate BibleZone® resources.
If you did not use a section, write "Did not use" in the Comments space.

1 = In No Lessons   2 = In Some Lessons   3 = In Most Lessons   4 = In All Lessons

1. *Enter the Zone* provided information that helped me teach this lesson's Scripture.
1   2   3   4   Comments:

2. The *Scope the Zone* chart made lesson planning easy.
1   2   3   4   Comments:

3. The teaching plan was organized in a way that made it easy to use.
1   2   3   4   Comments:

4. The Teacher's Guide provided easy-to-follow instructions for the learning activities.
1   2   3   4   Comments:

5. The supplies necessary to do the activities were easily located in my home or church.
1   2   3   4   Comments:

6. My students were able to understand the lesson's ZoneIn®.
1   2   3   4   Comments:

7. The activities matched the learning level and abilities of my students.
1   2   3   4   Comments:

8. The number of activities in the lesson plan worked for the time I had available (indicate how much time):_____.
If not, check:_____ too many _____too few.
1   2   3   4   Comments:

9. I used activities from the BirthdayZone section of the Teacher's Guide.
1   2   3   4   Comments:

10. I used activities from the SnackZone section of the Teacher's Guide.
1   2   3   4   Comments:

11. I used activities from the SongZone section of the Teacher's Guide.
1   2   3   4   Comments:

12. I used the Cassette in my classroom.
1   2   3   4   Comments:

13. I used items from the BibleZone® FUNspirational® Kit.
1   2   3   4   Comments:

14. I sent the HomeZone® page home to parents.
1   2   3   4   Comments:

15. I used the BZ Bee puppet with my class.
1   2   3   4   Comments:

ADDITIONAL COMMENTS

Activities my students enjoy the most are:

Activities my students enjoy the least are:

I use BibleZone® for_____Sunday School _____Second-Hour Sunday School _____Children's Church

_____Wednesday nights _____Sunday nights _____Children's Fellowship _____other

ABOUT MY CLASS

Number of children at each age in my class:

_____Age 3_____Age 4_____Age 5

_____Other (Specify)_____

Average number of children who attend my class each week:_____

I teach: _____alone _____with another teacher each week

_____taking turns with other teachers _____with an adult helper

ABOUT MY CHURCH

_____Rural _____Small Town _____Downtown _____Suburban

_____Under 200 Members _____200-700 Members _____Over 700 Members

Church Name and Address: _____

_____

My Name and Address: _____

_____

Please return this form to: **Amy Smith**
Research Department
201 8th Ave., So.
P.O. Box 801
Nashville, TN 37202-0801